Getting the Most Out of the Research Experience

Getting the Most Out of the Research Experience

What Every Researcher Needs to Know

Brian Roberts

SAGE Publications

Los Angeles • London • New Delhi • Singapore

2/25/08

SAGE Publications Ltd
1 Oliver's Yard
55 City Road
London EC1Y 1SP

SAGE Publications Inc.
2455 Teller Road
Thousand Oaks, California 91320

SAGE Publications India Pvt Ltd
B 1/I 1 Mohan Cooperative Industrial Area
Mathura Road, New Delhi 110 044
India

SAGE Publications Asia-Pacific Pte Ltd
33 Pekin Street #02-01
Far East Square
Singapore 048763

British Library Cataloguing in Publication data

A catalogue record for this book is available
from the British Library

ISBN 978 0 7619 4119 4
ISBN 978 0 7619 4120 0

Library of Congress control number 2006935818

Typeset by C&M Digitals (P) Ltd., Chennai, India
Printed and bound in Great Britain by Athenaeum Press, Gateshead
Printed on paper from sustainable resources

To Evan and Mary

CONTENTS

ACKNOWLEDGEMENTS

I would like to thank Professor Chris Rojek, who had the original idea, for his invitation to write the book. I am grateful to Sage for their patience and for the help I have received. I would like to thank Dr Peter Billing, Director, Center for Regional and Tourism Research, Bornholm, Denmark and Professor Mats Greiff, Head, History Studies, Malmö University, Sweden, who kindly invited me to visit and work in their institutions for several weeks during 2004 – I was treated with great hospitality and provided with a welcome opportunity to study. As usual, without the support of Mag, Rhiannon and Iwan I would not have finished this book.

1

THE RESEARCHER

Sociology is more like a passion. The sociological perspective is more like a demon that possesses one, that drives one compellingly, again and again, to the questions that are its own. (Berger, 1966: 36)

   The researcher experience is not just peripheral to the research and should thus have a place in the reporting of the research. We think it is time the researcher experience be given more prominence than just a discussion in doctoral seminars and as an add-on in presentations at some research conferences. (Moch and Gates, 2000a: 3)

The conduct of research

Students and researchers are often confused about their role in research, for instance, on questions of ethics, relations with respondents, issues of how to secure funding, submitting for publication and response to criticism. This book is intended to be an 'accessible' introduction to the experience of conducting research. It attempts to address the researcher's role – not as usual through a discussion of the methods used, but as an 'advice-cum-comforter' book on how to approach research. The kinds of subjective problem that researching produces, the ways to communicate research, the response to the sharing of research findings, including publications, and other practical issues are helpfully discussed. The objective is to outline the subjective 'side' of research as the researcher conducts research and communicates results. In this way, it is a grounded combination of the 'methodological' with actual research practice as it bears upon life contexts. At a time when there is time-pressure on the supervisory relationship between staff and research students and the increasing demands on researchers to initiate and complete research, this book should provide much needed support to the new and developing researcher.

Undergraduate and postgraduate students and researchers in the social sciences now have an excellent range of textbooks covering the span of research methods – on how to carry out the 'mechanics' of research or the step-by-step procedures of quantitative and, increasingly, qualitative research (see Bryman, 2004; May, 2001; Robson, 2002). There are also a number of comprehensive edited compilations of articles on broad areas and issues, in both qualitative (see Bryman and Burgess, 1994, 1999; Crabtree and Miller, 1999; and Denzin and Lincoln, 2000a) and quantita-tive research and analysis (see Kaplan, 2004), and also on 'mixed methods' (see Bryman, 2006). There are, of course, innumerable books on specific research methods, procedures and analyses (e.g. interviewing, the survey, participant observation, case studies, statistical analysis, and discourse). In short, students wanting authoritative guides to research – the applicability of various methods and statistical and other analyses – are not devoid of choice.

Traditional textbooks have not generally considered the 'role' of the researcher in sufficient depth to indicate the 'feelings' involved in research. The nearest method, perhaps, to give such a consideration is participant observation, where questions of 'entering the field' and fieldwork relations have figured prominently. However, in sociology, anthropology and related substantive areas, a re-evaluation has been taking place for some years on the researcher's role, with questions of self, power-relations and commit-ment coming to the fore. In this regard, feminist research and theory has played a particularly important part in questioning the researcher's role within forms of interviewing, participant observation, broader fieldwork and even wider, more quantitative research practices. This book draws on some of these changes and discussions, but by emphasising the practical implications for the student/researcher intending to undertake research – faced with choices, pitfalls, responsibilities, relations and so on in the research contexts and practice.

This book is therefore intended to provide a ready guide to the subjective and practical concerns met in the research and writing process. Many research texts do not have sufficient breadth in dealing with the 'subjective' aspects of research across all types of approach and the full length of the research process. Generally they do not describe in detail 'experiential-practical' issues, such as 'entering the field' and 'presentation/management', in terms of the relation between researcher and respondent. Some developments in research methodology have centred on a number of specific areas relevant to discussions of the researcher's reflection and biography. Certainly, there has been much discussion of issues such as the collaboration in research with those studied, and the possibilities for auto/ethnography and other 'self-writing' forms. But again, few sources fully engage with the issue of the researcher's role throughout the research process. One valuable text by Hallowell et al. (2005) gives some fascinating reports by numerous researchers reflecting on their emotions, self, others, control and ethics, but is not a detailed guide as such.

An important part of researcher experience is 'reflexivity'. Discussion of 'reflexivity' has generally centred on qualitative research practice, particularly due to an often close connection between researcher and 'subject' or context. Yet, an appreciation of the need to reflect on practice cannot be confined to qualitative procedures. In quantitative work there are research relations (although often limited) with respondents and colleagues, and non-research influences which require recognition and understanding. All researchers engaged in whatever method or procedure are active, experiencing beings who meet triumphs as well as difficulties in the routines of daily living. An intensive discussion of the various meanings of 'reflexivity' is more than is intended here. More prosaically, the focus will be on forms of 'monitoring' of action in research – what does and can take place in the active research life of the researcher in relation to material collected and the research context. It is not intended in this book to explore in detail 'experience' in existential, phenomenological or other terms, or to compare and contrast particular approaches and 'claims' (e.g. in varieties of feminist methodology and theory). Rather, the task is more 'immediate' – to give an indication of likely research experience and, without being too formulaic or prescriptive, provide a guide to coping with research difficulties while pointing to the 'positives' (e.g. the enjoyment and sense of achievement) of research. In summary, research practice is not to be seen as simply about the application of techniques, methodology and analysis. It is also about the researcher learning about, and reflecting on, the personal intricacies and social situation of the research process.

In short, the book aims to be a practical, helpful guide to an area relatively neglected in research methods textbooks – the researcher's experience of research. Included here is what to expect in research – not simply the negative, but also the positive challenges of carrying out a study – whether it be by interviews on others, survey work, in the research archive or some other activity. It is meant to be a source of guidance, 'comfort' and help to the student and researcher. While many of the references are made to 'sociologists' and 'sociology', the discussion is also relevant to the broader social sciences. There is a need for a book that describes and answers such practical, subjective issues in research, not merely for qualitative research, where many of these issues have been raised, but also in quantitative research. Also, certain kinds of research, such as documentary and other forms of secondary research, must not be forgotten on this issue. The core audience for the text is final-year students undertaking courses in research methods and preparing for and undertaking a final-year dissertation, postgraduate thesis students, and less experienced researchers. Of course, 'research' takes place in various forms and by many organisations outside the university (see Finnegan, 2005), but here the focus is upon the academic context.

What is research?

A key initial question is what constitutes 'research'? What is meant by 'research'? At least in the UK, universities increasingly wish to distinguish those who are deemed 'research active' from among their staff. 'Research', in fact, can cover quite a wide range of activities with sometimes a separation made between 'research' and 'scholarship'. 'Research active' would include the publication of research, gaining funds, and supervision and examination of postgraduate research students. It could also include organising conferences, refereeing articles for journals, and grant applications, being on an editorial board, and being a member of research committees of professional organisations. Scholarship, on the other hand, may include course development, writing book reviews and textbooks, undergraduate external examining, conference attendance, being active in a professional body, acting as a book editor and contributing articles to non-professional publications (e.g. newspapers), and as including technological advances or creative artistic works, or consultancy roles, or even new teaching modes. More restrictively, 'research' in this book will be used to refer to the study of substantive issues and theoretical questions by the application of one or more research methods, and the interpretation and dissemination of 'findings'.

Research can be considered as a process rather than a single event; it is often likened to a 'journey' by the researcher (Roberts, 2004). It is 'a process that demands planning, forethought, commitment, and persistence. In fact, research is more of a journey than a task; and like any journey, it needs to be managed, navigated, and negotiated from early conception to final destination' (O'Leary, 2004: 15). The notion of research as a journey does not mean that it is a mere sightseeing trip or a guided tour, even if these involve observation and some reflection – and can involve a degree of stamina! In an investigation, detailed observation and reflection are essential ingredients, and the physical demands of research can be high. In my own study in south Wales I remember struggling on foot up a rough track on dark, rainy winter nights to where I was staying in a farm house after interviewing in the local town. Research is a journey of self-knowledge and, at least to some extent, 'a way of life'.

Engagement in a study has effects on non-research life. For instance, we often refer to our research in non-academic contexts and in 'ordinary conversations' with others when they ask what we have been doing, or enquire of its progress. A discussion or a news item may well raise an issue which has a bearing on what we have researched. So, it is not only for the period when we have planned, carried out and reported our project, our activities also have a wider biographical 'relevance'. In this sense, 'the research' has a wider and longer effect on us than is often thought. We can find ourselves thinking about it or referring to it, sometimes unexpectedly, in various situations. In giving a lecture or seminar, we may use it as an anecdote, an illustration or as an aside. It may feature in a later setting to establish our credentials as someone who can speak 'about research' having carried some out, or to show to others and society more generally that we are 'useful' and deserve our rewards. In conversation, we may refer to what we have done or even claim some 'legitimacy' for what we are saying – 'When I was doing my research, I found that …'.

While research is often seen as a 'journey', in my view, it can be further understood as an 'adventure':

> In an adventure there is, in place of the involuntary routinization of *time*, a voluntary departure from the mundane world. *Space* is reorganized and reconstructed in an adventure so that its essence is experienced in the open territories, interstices, or reconstituted areas of the ordinary world. Finally, *manner* (or 'self') is inverted or perverted: the adventure permits man [*sic*] to assume new identities, adopt different styles, improvise on untried themes, and in general, prove untested mettle. (Lyman and Scott, 1984: 182–3)

A rather idealised view, containing something of sociological practice as an adventure, is held by Berger:

> The sociologist, at his [*sic*] best, is a man with a taste for other lands, inwardly open to the measureless richness of human possibilities, eager for new horizons and new worlds of human meaning. It probably requires no additional elaboration to make the point that this type of man can play a particularly useful part in the course of events today. (Berger, 1966: 67)

This conception, although rather 'romantic', does give an idea of the excitement of social investigation and a sense of 'discovery'. There is the exhilaration of the 'quest' of finding something new. Research can also be likened to an adventure in that while the end of the research is earmarked by deadlines and particular results may be expected, there is an 'openness' found not only in forms of fieldwork research, where it is encouraged, but even in more traditional survey methods.

The research 'adventure' and its context

While likening research to an 'adventure' it must be borne in mind that a wide range of factors may influence the researcher's actions, including funding, research relationships, personal attachments, values and ethics, and so on. These can both constrain and guide practice:

The following groups may impinge on the sociologist's actions: clients, subjects, respondents, informants, research organizations, granting agencies, academic communities, students, colleagues, scientific and professional societies, and even local, national, and international political communities. ... A consideration of values and ethics in sociology must answer first this question: to whom are sociologists accountable when they make observations? My position is that they are responsible to many differing pressure groups. (Denzin, 1970: 326, 332)

What is a 'researcher'?

The role of 'researcher' is one of a number of activities that can be assigned to the sociologist. The traditional investigative stance within sociology is informed by the idea of the 'objective researcher', who skilfully explores, in a detached manner, a particular question or (often pressing) social issue. Rather differently, the sociologist is someone with 'an agenda' relevant to social change:

... who wishes to emancipate, liberate, and work towards sometimes radical change. ... The nature of agenda-based research means that subjectivities take on a key role in the research process, and are managed only to the extent that they are made transparent and do not bias data analysis. The goals, aims, and objectives of this type of research need to articulate both the knowledge that is likely to result from the process, as well as the researcher's agenda for change. Similarly, the background and rationale of the study should clearly show the positioning of the researcher. Others can then be in a position to critically evaluate the nature and credibility of the knowledge produced, given named agendas and subjectivities. (O'Leary, 2004: 59)

The recommendation of 'clarity' regarding the position of the researcher should apply to all kinds of sociological and broader social science research.

The consideration of research practice and its connection with an 'agenda' led (since at least the 1960s) to an examination of its political context. Becker (1967) famously posed the question 'Whose side are we on?' when undertaking research. He argued that it is not possible to research without 'personal and political sympathies' intruding:

> … the question is not whether we should take sides, since we inevitably will, but rather whose side are we on. … In the greatest variety of subject matter areas and in work done by all the different methods at our disposal, we cannot avoid taking sides, for reasons firmly based in social structure. (Becker, 1967: 239)

Nicolaus famously argued that due to the increasingly expensive nature of social research, those who took part were 'compelled' to reach to the 'civil, military, and economic sovereignty' to 'prove themselves "useful"' – a 'social fact' that was fundamental to 'any understanding of the politics of the organized sociological profession' (Nicolaus, 1972: 51):

> In the post-war era the road to prominence, hence office, within the profession has been paved with research publication. Once he [sic] obtains financing for a research venture, the sociologist builds up, through publication, his professional reputation. This form of capital is then convertible into academic promotion, which yields better access to more research funds, permitting further publication, yielding further promotion, even closer proximity to the big money, and so on up, until, as supervisor of graduate students, the successful sociological entrepreneur is in a position to start and manage younger persons on the same spiral. The inevitable consequence of this career-pattern, if ability is held constant, is to reward servility. The structure is such that the achievement of prominence in the profession is a direct function of the decisions of outside financial powers. (Nicolaus, 1972: 51)

The important point here, whether or not we fully accept Nicolaus's radical view, is the need to place the sociologist's experience and practice within its socio-political setting. Giddens, for example, in a somewhat more anxious mode, points to the centrality of sociology in having both a broader understanding of social life as well as its vital role in current circumstances:

> The sociological enterprise is now even more pivotal to the social sciences as a whole, and indeed to current intellectual culture generally, than it has ever been before. We live today, not to put too fine a point on it, in a world on a knife-edge between extraordinary possibility and global disaster. (Giddens, 1987: 17)

Finally, while research can be seen as an adventure, albeit in a changing political and societal context, it is also 'craft' that is part of the wider field of academic work:

Scholarship is a choice of how to live as well as a choice of career; whether he [sic] knows it or not, the intellectual workman forms his own self as he works towards the perfection of his craft; to realize his own potentialities, and any opportunities that come his way, he constructs a character which has as its core the qualities of the good workman. (Mills, 1970: 216)

Images of sociology and the sociologist

Prospective students usually give an 'interest in people' as informing their decision to study sociology, or that the subject will enable them to help people, or inform social policy, social reform or social work. In broad terms, the reasons given for study centre on wanting to find out more about an area of social concern. Ultimately students want their endeavours to have some social value. However, there are a number of other conceptions or 'images' of sociology, and some of them are very pejorative – as a pointless activity squandering funds for research that could be better used elsewhere or using 'fancy' language to describe what we all know from 'common sense'. Of course, some of the views of sociology and its research may have a degree of truth because of an over-elaboration of theories and some research may not be particularly 'valuable'.

In terms of social research, the sociologist is sometimes described as a kind of 'technicist' concerned with the intricacies of research methodology or a compiler of social statistics (a kind of demographer) especially on pressing social issues. These conceptions are traditional views related to the pursuit of sociology as a 'science' (Berger, 1966: 22–3). Further views conceive sociology as a 'critical' activity, seeing society with the eye of an outsider (with some detachment), who observes the bustle of daily life and holds up its absurdities, injustices, and unintended outcomes as well as its 'humanity' for comment. Perhaps, unlike Berger, I would not stress the term 'science' so fully, but otherwise I would agree with the following:

The sociologist, then, is someone concerned with understanding society in a disciplined way. The nature of this discipline is scientific. This means that what the sociologist finds and says about the social phenomena he studies occurs within a certain rather strictly defined frame of reference. (Berger, 1966: 27)

In doing so, the sociologist 'will have to be concerned with the exact significance of the terms' being used and their meaning, while also being someone who is 'intensively, endlessly, shamelessly interested in the doings' of people (Berger, 1966: 28, 29). While Berger gives priority to the role of theorisation and understanding for its own sake, 'research', in its broadest sense, we can argue, as exploring, gaining information and assessing material, is ultimately very much involved in the processes of theorisation. The sociologist may be seen in a further 'reflective' biographical light. For example, sociologists of the Chicago School, such as Robert Park and W.I. Thomas, were very aware of the transition they had made from small-town, rural backgrounds to become part of a bustling, rapidly growing twentieth-century city. Their personal migration – within the migration of millions of others – was a main concern, not simply for the social difficulties created for groups, but also for the individual effects, including on their own outlook (see Park, 1928). It is this view of the sociologist reflecting on his or her own social settings, work activities and life transitions in relation to wider social processes to which I have the greatest sympathy and attachment.

Within sociology (and many social and natural science disciplines) much discussion had taken place in recent years on how to change common images of research work. The intention has been to show the benefits of research and wider study, and relay findings through the media and in a manner which will not undergo undue simplification according to certain 'sensationalist' news values. Academia has become increasingly aware of the 'value' of PR and the requirements of the 'market place'. This is reflected in the publicity given to research delivered at conferences or reported in journals. Public and private sponsors increasingly want the research they support to have an 'impact' – a media visibility which can affect the public and impress other organisations, including governments. The 'dissemination' of findings, often rather overlooked in the past, has become an increasingly important part of the 'research process' rather than an afterthought. For various reasons, therefore, academics have become more aware of the public context, and anxious to dispel common portrayals of academic research as self-indulgent, obscure, non-practical and jargon-laden. There is a need to establish the 'legitimacy' of research and to overcome the at least perceived disjunction between academic and public discourses on the nature of sociological and other research practices.

Research roles and researcher characteristics

From monk to salesperson?

The researcher in sociology has a much wider set of roles and requires a broader set of abilities than most textbooks on 'methods' allow for. At times the researcher will feel more like a monk or a prisoner, contemplating alone the research activity being undertaken in an unfamiliar setting – perhaps spending time in hotels while 'in the field'. In fact, research can be quite a lonely experience outside the academic department as one tries to make contacts, gain 'access' to different organisations or situations, and establish oneself, in relation to others, as a 'researcher'. The informants/subjects will also have expectations of the researcher that have to be considered. For instance, in my own fieldwork research in Wales, I was often introduced by 'locals' as a 'writer' of a book on the area. At other points in the research I felt more like a salesperson, (uneasily) portraying the research and myself to an audience. Commonly, at the point of dissemination, it does often feel as if you are 'selling', and if you have written a book, of course, you are drawn into the publisher's sales campaign – you become a 'publicist'! At other times you feel like an entrepreneur seeking out opportunities – in putting forward your proposal for funds, giving a presentation on your research, in 'selling' your 'product'. It can be said that academic life generally is increasingly drawn into more commercial modes of operation.

After days spent poring over statistical results, transcribing interviews, making copious notes, assembling folders of materials, and weeks writing the research report, articles or book, research can seem a 'monkish' experience unless effort is made to break out and meet people! After the research is completed, it seems as though the experience was already long ago and has been turned into a 'performance' for conferences or even as part of presentations for more funds – again, a 'selling' of what has been done, or will be done. Research 'output' then seems to have become a 'commodity' which is justified according to 'objective' parameters by funders and evaluators, to be graded and audited. In this way, more funds are received and reputations established.

What the researcher needs

Apart from the general administrative skills, researchers must obtain a range of 'technical' abilities (e.g. in collating materials, in using methods such as questionnaire survey, and in means of interpretation) as well as an awareness of various methodological issues (e.g. questions regarding research ethics, access and dissemination). But, there are also various 'characteristics' which the researcher has to develop as part of the research activities. These include:

- patience
- stamina
- perseverance
- openness
- inquisitiveness
- discretion
- humour
- insight
- sensitivity
- organisation

Above all, 'reflection' is the most important characteristic needed by a researcher. It is not merely a feature associated with what are usually conceived as the 'technicalities' of methodology, but with the fuller life as a researcher – as part of interacting with others in a variety of research and related non-research settings. In short, we can advise the 'researcher – know thyself'!

Main aims

The aim of the book is to provide a discussion of the subjective aspects of research activities. It offers a lively guide to how to meet research problems by providing examples of research and hints and tips. In addition to advice and help, the book aims to be a source of reassurance for the researcher – a supportive framework for the researcher facing the 'subjective life' of the research process. It aims to bridge the gap between the piles of research 'guide books' and the 'actual' research that is intended or already underway.

Chapter outlines

Chapter 2, 'Researcher Styles, Roles and Contexts', considers the different styles of research and their status. It asks the prospective researcher to examine what it is to be a researcher and its personal importance. A number of practical issues which impinge on researcher experience are discussed, including how research ideas come about, networking and the search for funds, as well as how research relations are affected by the different social settings in which research takes place.

Chapter 3, 'The "Emotional" Aspects of Research', examines the 'subjective' side of research and how the researcher can cope with research difficulties. It argues that research involves 'emotional labour', a 'reflexivity', and the employment of a number of 'life skills'. Questions regarding collaboration with others and necessary sources of subjective support are raised, especially in relation to 'maintaining momentum' and dealing with anxiety and stress when they occur.

Chapter 4, 'Entering the Research: The Presentation of the Researcher's Self', begins by examining the reasons for a study and the entrance to research. An argument is offered for the role of 'sociological imagination' and for a fuller recognition of the interconnections of research with our 'daily lives'. The chapter addresses the 'hold-ups' of research and how to meet them. It also discusses the nature of the 'PhD experience' and how such postgraduate study should be approached.

Chapter 5, 'Interpretation in Research', introduces the researcher as interpreter and theorist within the conduct of research as a whole, and not simply during the collection and understanding of materials. It discusses the research diary, in which the investigator can record notes on his or her personal life as well as observations and insights that can be a form of 'self-analysis' and a source for later reflection. Such notes play an important part in informing the 'writing-up' of the report. The chapter outlines the difficulties and the satisfactions that arise in interpreting materials and how interpretations and new ideas can be organised.

Chapter 6, 'Writing Research', points out that the researcher is also an author who is writing for an audience. Considered here are the nature of academic writing, working with others, and researcher autobiographies and 'confessions' of research practice. The chapter also considers the writing process in relation to identity and how to prepare for writing.

Chapter 7, 'Dissemination', examines what is meant by 'dissemination'. It considers the different audiences for research findings, including those researched, funding bodies and the media. Also included is an outline of the various forms of dissemination, for example the doctoral thesis, research report or briefing, conference papers, book and journal articles, books, the internet and in teaching, and how these are undertaken. In all of these, it is argued, the 'biographical self' of the researcher is implicated.

'Reactions to Research', the subject of Chapter 8, can vary a great deal. As an example, feedback to authors articles in submitting and receiving decisions by editors is examined. The researcher 'invests' a large part of him or herself in the research process. It is not surprising, therefore, that the reactions of others can, at different times, have a deflating or an uplifting effect. In writing an article, book or report, and in giving a presentation, the researcher exposes him or herself to others' responses. It can therefore be a time of vulnerability but also of personal reward.

After the completion of research and the writing up, if not before, the question arises of what is the next step? More research? The pursuit of a broader academic career? Or something entirely different? Of course, the research may be part of an existing career plan and be part of personal development in a professional occupation outside academia. Chapter 9, 'What Next in My Research?', returns to the questions of researcher roles and identity, and how the research is to be fitted into the CV and future career.

As a summary, Chapter 10, 'Conclusion: The Researcher's Experience of Research', considers the research experience again in terms of emotions, the biography of the researcher, researcher identity and insights that the research 'adventure' can bring in relation to the researcher's self.

Key points to remember on researcher experience

Points to keep in mind before, during and after research include the following:

- While research is part of your life, do not let it rule it!
- Research brings responsibilities to those you research, and obligations to colleagues, the researched, funders, family and friends, and perhaps to society as a whole.
- To be a researcher is to be curious, inquiring and reflective.
- You do not have to like people, but you should find them interesting!
- Research is an adventure – not as a reckless, unplanned exercise, but a period of discovery.

Summary

As a researcher, I am most drawn to a notion of research not simply as the application of 'methods', but as a practice that can be likened to an adventure – a series of new relationships, of new 'things' found, and as a period of self-discovery. This chapter has outlined a number of issues in the research process which will be explored further in subsequent chapters. In summary, the position taken on research practice is as follows:

- The research experience is integral to the conduct of research.
- The research process is part of the biographical life of the researcher.
- The researcher brings expectations, anxieties and hopes to a study, and experiences a wide range of feelings during the research process.
- The researcher and the researched share a human situation as biographical actors.

Further reading

N. Hallowell et al. (eds) (2005) *Reflections on Research* (Maidenhead: Open University Press) is an interesting compilation of comments (on emotions, self, others, control and ethics) by a wide range of researchers on their previous research. An older study which looks at the interconnections between research activities and the private life of the researcher is J. Platt (1976) *Realities of Social Research.* (London: Sussex University Press/Chatto and Windus). L. Blaxter et al. (2001) *How to Research* (2nd edn, Buckingham: Open University Press) is a very informative, step-by-step guide to the research process using exercises, boxes and extensive further reading; it is a very practical text but is not so much slanted towards the experience of research – the anxieties and problems and how to deal with them. Another useful text is A. Coffey's (1999) *The Ethnographic Self* (London:

Sage), which reflects recent discussion of the researcher in ethnographic work without the more practical remit required here. H.S. Becker's (1998) *Tricks of the Trade: How To Think about Your Research While You're Doing It* (Chicago: University of Chicago Press) is informative and useful, but is focused on more theoretical-methodological concerns and again does not have the more 'accessible' form and style adopted in this text. On researcher experience in a number of research contexts, see S.D. Moch and M.F. Gates (eds) (2000b) *The Researcher Experience in Qualitative Research* (London: Sage). A number of 'readers' on research methods, commonly in qualitative research, draw attention to researcher experience to some extent. For example, see D. Silverman (2000) *Doing Qualitative Research: A Practical Handbook* (London: Sage) Chapters 2–3 for accounts by research students, while C. Seale et al. (eds) (2004) *Qualitative Research Practice* (London: Sage), contains some chapters which take a 'somewhat autobiographical approach' which cautions against too confessional an approach. There are very many practical texts which have some relevance. For instance, see G. Birley and N. Moreland (1998) *A Practical Guide to Academic Research* (London: Kogan Page); A. Fink (2005) *Conducting Research Literature Reviews* (2nd edn, London: Sage); M. Denscombe (2003) *The Good Research Guide* (2nd edn, Buckingham: Open University Press); B. Hawkins and M. Sorgi (1985) *Research: How To Plan, Speak and Write about it* (Berlin/ New York: Springer Verlag); L.F. Locke et al. (1993) *Proposals That Work* (3rd edn, London: Sage); and N.S.R. Walliman (2000) *Your Research Project* (London: Sage). Blaxter et al. (1998), *The Academic Career Handbook* (Buckindam: Open University Press) has a good discussion and offers advice on areas such as networking and getting published, and other elements of an academic career.

2

RESEARCH STYLES, ROLES AND CONTEXTS

Just how and why I decided to do such a study [on the elite] may suggest one way in which one's life experiences feed one's intellectual work. (Mills, 1970: 220)

The scientific procedures used by the sociologist imply some specific values that are peculiar to this discipline. One such value is the careful attention to matters that other scholars might consider pedestrian and unworthy of the dignity of being objects of scientific investigation – something one might almost call a democratic focus of interest in the sociological approach. (Berger, 1966: 188)

Sociologists are no more ready than other men [*sic*] to cast a cold eye on their own doings. No more than others are they ready, willing, or able to tell us what they are really doing and to distinguish this firmly from what they *should* be doing. ... The historical mission of a Reflexive Sociology as I conceive it, however, would be to *transform* the sociologist, to penetrate deeply into his daily life and work, enriching them with new sensitivities, and to raise the sociologist's self-awareness to a new historical level. (Gouldner, 1972, in Seale, 2004: 381–2)

Styles of research – qualitative and quantitative research experience

'Research' encompasses a very broad set of 'styles' and 'methodologies' in the collection of materials or data, and particular methods and substantive issues shift in 'popularity' over time. It can be more 'open' or 'exploratory' in methodological design, or apply strict procedures to 'test' an 'hypothesis'. Research methods can be broadly placed within quantitative or qualitative approaches, and a study may be 'large scale' or 'small scale', short-term or long-term, and may have many or few numbers of those researched (see Silverman, 2000: Chapter 1). Research practice may also focus on more secondary or documentary sources or deal directly with 'subjects', as in interviewing. Research can take place in one or many locations – some far afield and involving the excitement or inconvenience of travel. Also, if far away, certainly for extended periods, research practice can be associated with loneliness due to the separation from home and colleagues, and the familiarities of place and culture. Such feelings of homesickness for the researcher may even occur if he or she is part of a team in the research setting. Fortunately, today it is much easier to keep in contact with home and the research 'base' by direct phone or the internet, but physical distance can still have an effect. A researcher, of course, may also take part in several types of research procedure and in a variety of settings even within the same research study. The various forms of relationship with those studied may differ in terms of duration and closeness of involvement (some fleeting, as in simple response questionnaires; some perhaps leading to quite deep personal involvement, as in participant observation). How to act according to different research relations can raise questions of 'simple' good manners and respect, through to deeper ethical, possibly legal, and other issues in terms of responsibilities to all those involved. Professional bodies commonly have codes of practice to guide researchers on these issues (e.g. BSA, see Seale, 2004). Sociological endeavour can also bring differing types of relationship with other research colleagues – as supervisor or student, employer or employed, and collaborator.

A further distinction associated with the researcher's approach can be made between the scientific principles of the 'positivistic' tradition in the social sciences and the increasingly strong alternative approaches which have challenged the traditional criteria for research practice and investigative methodologies (see Denzin and Lincoln, 2000a). The traditional or positivistic approach has important implications for the researcher stance and experience. In this view, the investigator is essentially someone who is a technician or a trained, qualified expert in a certain field, who examines a subject with detachment and objectivity. Personal life, attitudes, preferences and feelings are to be 'bracketed off' from research practice. Hypotheses are to be tested by the gathering of 'facts'. The 'ideal' stance is one of non-emotionality; research is a clinical exercise. The positivist researcher is essentially an observer and measurer of the social 'reality'. In contrast, the 'post-positivist' researcher has a very different orientation – to a social world that is seen as fluid, complex, and perhaps ungraspable, with differing notions of truth and multiple 'realities'.

> Post-positivists believe that the traditional gap between the researcher and the researched is one that can (and should) be diminished. ... Researchers can act in ways that are: *participatory and collaborative* – rather than research focusing solely *on* a particular group, post-positivist researchers can also work both *for* and *with* participants; and *subjective* – researchers acknowledge being value-bound. They admit to biases that can affect their studies. The question for post-positivist researchers is how to recognize and manage, and in some situations, even-value and use subjectivities endemic to the research process. (O'Leary, 2004: 6–7)

Forms of research

A research project can take many forms: it may include one or more techniques (e.g. interview, questionnaire); it can take place in very different settings and over varying lengths of time; and it can be conducted by one or more researchers.

The general purpose of research is to gain information and pursue understanding in a consistent, clear, understandable and rigorous manner. Research can be:

- An investigation of an issue or problem
- Application of a theory or theories
- Testing a specific hypothesis
- Participatory (with a Group or community)
- Related to policy formation
- Gathering together existing research data.

Blaxter says that numerous types of research or accounts of research share certain 'basic characteristics'; they 'are, or aim to be, planned, cautious, systematic and reliable ways of finding out or deepening understanding' (Blaxter et al., 2001: 5).

Whatever the research stance, qualitative or quantitative in broad approach, a very important point here is the sense of well-being and security which flows from having a well-defined research role. There is some desire or 'need to position' oneself as a certain kind of researcher and identify with a 'defined way of knowing' – we become attached and socialised in a particular personal orientation and experience (O'Leary, 2004: 8). We tend to feel most comfortable with a certain mode of operating and self-definition, as having perceived 'strengths' as a particular kind of investigator.

The conduct of research is often outlined as a simple chronological process with an emphasis on the gathering of the data by either qualitative and/or quantitative methods. However, the research process is more lengthy and complex than often described:

Doing sociology is not just about selecting and constructing a data collection technique. On the contrary, it embraces conceptualization of the problem, theoretical debate, specification of research practices, analytic frameworks, and epistemological presuppositions. Data collection is not a self-contained phase in a linear process. Rather, all aspects of the research process are interrelated and all bear on each other. There is no neat linear sequence of events as the idealized research report format would have us believe (i.e. theoretical background, hypothesis, design of research instrument, data collection, test of hypothesis, findings, and implications for theory). However much the idealized form of research design and presentation might be imposed on other forms of research, dialectical critical social research is not conducive to such manipulation. (Harvey, 1990: 208)

On the face of it, 'quantitative' research, at least for some potential practitioners, may appear dry, boring and routinised, and it does have its more mundane tasks. For instance, it can involve the administration of questionnaires, or waiting for the return of envelopes from a mail questionnaire – with any pleasure at receipt and thought of a good response rate tempered by the thought of more data input. Data analysis can seem a mountain to climb when faced with columns and rows of statistical data, formulae and test results to disentangle, requiring seemingly endless days at the computer desk processing the findings. 'Qualitative' work may have the aura of less certainty and seem to be more exciting – the researcher 'in the field' having a different, even more romantic persona than the 'methodological-technicist' in the research room, or the documentary researcher in the archive. Nevertheless, quantitative research strategies do have their pleasures and satisfactions:

Now I have a real love-hate relationship with quantitative data and statistics. All the numbers, coding, data entry, stats programs, knowing what tests to run, and understanding the meaning of various p-values ... can be a nightmare. The pay off, however, is that if this is done with diligence and rigour, you come out with this beautiful thing called 'statistical significance'. You actually get numbers that assess the reliability/validity/ generalizability of your findings. (O'Leary, 2004: 114)

Qualitative research, while it can seem initially 'easier' and more interesting, also has its routines and chores, and contains doubts about what may be found. Increasingly, it involves the computer 'lab' as more qualitative research computer programs are adopted. Often qualitative and quantitative research techniques may be used together in a research project, although in varying degrees. Even so, the common view in discussions of research methods is that there is a rigid distinction between practices. On the one hand, there is the immersion of the researcher in the context with a close interaction with the 'subjects', and on the other, there are practices in which there is an 'objective' stance that separates the researcher from those studied. At the most simple, it is usually held, in the one practice there is the reporting of the 'facts', in the other, the information regarding social life emerges in the interactive context of research itself.

At the centre of recent methodological discussion has been a re-evaluation of the epistemological assumptions of research practice, including a fuller and more positive appreciation of the researcher's role, especially in relation to 'knowledge'. It is increasingly argued that researchers must take into account methodological and epistemological issues regarding how research 'knowledge' is produced in a context. This raises issues surrounding ethics, power, negotiation and the political dimensions of practice. Researchers, it is argued, must be aware of their own 'worldview' and their 'reality' in terms of power relations and the need to make these apparent (O'Leary, 2004: 43).

The status and stance of styles of research

Different types of research in sociology and other social sciences (and various topics of study) have different statuses that can vary over time. For a long time qualitative research methods were seen as less 'scientific'; at most, a lesser tradition. The use of methodological approaches such as ethnography and life histories were regarded as marginal – either more the province of anthropology or merely of interest to formulate some questions or ideas before the 'real job' of research got under way. In short, qualitative methods were seen as not fitting the rigours of scientific principles, such as reliability, validity, and sampling procedures. Major methodological textbooks tended to reflect this marginal status of qualitative methods, either by complete omission or by giving them little space. More recently, this position has changed. There has been a tremendous growth and development of qualitative work, featuring alongside more 'traditional' methods in major compendiums on methods and issues, and specific volumes are now devoted to a particular method. The 'rise' of qualitative methods has been associated with their growing acceptance and perhaps a greater self-regard and belief by practitioners.

Textbook roles

Textbook roles of the researcher tend to depict him or her as applying one or more research technique's in a prescribed manner as an 'interviewer', 'participant observer' or a 'surveyor'. However, such guides are not enough – they are inevitably limited accounts of research experience, focusing on one part or parts of the research process (traditionally, usually data collection) and cannot anticipate what can actually take place in the conduct of research. For example, working with other researchers can be very creative, and such collaboration on a project can produce a larger and more sophisticated piece of work, with insights and ideas that the single researcher would not have produced. However, relationships can at times go wrong; they can be frustrating since finding agreement may be difficult. Tensions can arise if it is felt someone in the team is not 'pulling their weight'. Bullying and harassment can even occur, leading to a breakdown in relations and even institutional grievance or other procedures being implemented. Textbook roles tend to be 'idealised' accounts of 'what should happen'.

Usually, in quantitative research the researcher's relationship with those being studied is quite transient or perhaps non-existent. The collection of data may take place over an extended period but the relation with each person is (at most) short-lived, even if a study involves meeting the same people on several occasions, as in longitudinal surveys and before-and-after experiments (Bryman, 1988). Some quantitative methods may not involve direct contact with participants, as in the conduct of mail questionnaires. Surveys and interviews may well be undertaken by other researchers on the team or by individuals (or an organisation) especially employed to undertake the task of gaining information from respondents. Nevertheless, although fleeting contact with respondents is usually a feature of quantitative research, it is important not to overlook the fact that the individual researcher is still involved – the research has a 'biographical experience', with feelings towards the research process, conceptions of the participants, and attitudes towards the material collected. Respondents may be viewed in a certain 'typical' light, the material may have been frustratingly difficult to collect, organise and interpret, and the whole process may have taken more or less time than anticipated. Participant observation and some forms of interview are carried out with intense contact, at least with some of the researched: 'For qualitative researchers, it is only by getting close to their subjects and becoming an insider that they can view the world as a participant in that setting' (Bryman, 1988: 96). In contrast, the traditional stance of the quantitative researcher is that of an 'outsider looking in on the social world': 'He or she applies a pre-ordained framework on the subjects being investigated and is involved as little as possible in that world' (Bryman, 1988: 96).

There are, of course, other forms of research in which contact with 'subjects' is 'indirect'. Unobtrusive measures, for example, can involve a very wide compass, including the study of formal (public) or informal (personal) records, visual imagery (photographs, videos), internet sources, graffiti and street rubbish (see Lee, 2000; Webb et al., 1966). In documentary research, the original 'subjects' and compilers may no longer be living. But, there is still the daily 'experience' of the researcher, who may well be affected by the sometimes dramatic and disturbing materials accessed and, although now 'distant', may well feel or have a responsibility to those 'voices', who may be no longer alive. Whatever the kind of research, the researcher has responsibilities, and associated feelings, in terms of a commitment to open research and maintaining the standards of the discipline, including accurate reporting and respect for the interests of participants or others whom the research may affect.

Responsibilities of the researcher

Researchers in all types of research have a number of responsibilities – to participants, colleagues, employer, funding body and to the furtherance of social knowledge. When they start research, sociologists and other researchers begin a set of relationships which entail responsibilities, obligations and feelings:

- There is the commitment to add to knowledge of the social world – this can be interpreted as a general obligation towards social betterment.
- The researcher starts a set of relationships with individuals and groups – the researched and others – that include ethical considerations.
- While committed to complete the research and advance knowledge, the legal and moral rights of others must be considered and respected.
- The obligations to funders, the department, the research team and others should not override the legal and moral rights of those who are being studied.
- The researcher has responsibilities related to how the material is written up, disseminated and its future usage.
- The researcher may well have ongoing, direct obligations towards those who have been studied (see British Sociological Association website and Seale, 2004).

The research method and topic chosen have a bearing on how we wish to be perceived by others, and how we see ourselves and our career hopes. The aspiring researcher is made aware of the areas that are receiving funding, are given higher 'status', or are methodologically and theoretically developing. We also wish our research to be seen as interesting by those in our wider intellectual and research community, and that it is going to be evaluated favourably in terms of our skills, the topicality of the research, or the insights made.

How important is being a researcher to you?

If we accept that research involves our biography, that it is part of our daily life and that we invest in it a great deal of ourselves, then its importance has a number of aspects. We may have chosen a subject or research theme that is close to our hearts, or perhaps it deals with a pressing social issue that concerns us and is in need of investigation. While undertaking research we may make certain sacrifices in terms of time that was already allotted to other activities, and perhaps 'cut corners' on outside personal commitments. The research we engage in can take on a personal importance. We may use it to 'identify' ourselves to others, for instance, as the person who has undertaken a certain kind of research on interesting and possibly important issues. In addition, it can be very flattering to be called an expert on a particular issue to a lay audience, or to be regarded as an authority on a methodology or research area by colleagues, and to be asked to give papers, review books, and evaluate research proposals for national bodies in our chosen field.

Where do research topics come from?

Ideas for research are traditionally seen as arising from other research, from a theoretical formulation, or from social policy issues. But, in fact, it is often unclear why we study a particular topic or research context. Formal reasons may be given in the research report, but there may be more practical reasons for such decisions, such as convenience of a location and time available. We may decide to take a topic according to our previous knowledge, or because of the degree to which we feel more or less 'comfortable' when entering the setting, or asking certain kinds of question. We may simply have researched in the setting before. Perhaps we choose to research a topic or a setting because it may give us some standing in the profession: it is a fashionable area receiving attention from funders; it is likely to attract approval from our colleagues; or the method to be used has become popular or is seen as innovative. Some other research topic may be seen as declining in importance, as not exciting, or the methodology may be seen as rather staid and unlikely to enable us to find something 'new' (Kleinman and Copp, 1993: 4–6).

The starting point for a research idea can be more connected to the broad life experiences of the researcher – an inquisitiveness or awareness – involving a desire to make connections, to delve deeper into the surrounding world. Less commonly, although found in feminist and some other perspectives, is the notion that the research question derives from or is connected with the biographical experience of the researcher. Thus, as Mills argues, an important aspect of the 'sociological imagination' is the realisation of the connection between 'private troubles' and 'public issues' (Mills, 1970). Reading research texts and reports, therefore, is only part of a wider set of influences (including the availability of funds) on the researcher's decision to investigate a substantive area or use a particular method.

Networking: research as market/research as friendship

An important aspect of research is 'networking' or making contact (by verbal communication, letter, telephone/texting, internet/email) with those in the same field. The idea of networking has sometimes been critically portrayed as ingratiating oneself with others and seeking some personal advantage. Certainly there are instances of such kinds of behaviour in academic life as in other areas. At least for less experienced researchers, there is sometimes a fear of being seen in such a self-interested light. However, networking can also be seen as a much more convivial and sharing activity, where the researchers exchange advice and information, discuss particular findings, or explore aspects of research procedure. Younger researchers in particular should not be afraid of making contacts, even with distinguished academics in the same field. If a response from a contact is not forthcoming or off-putting, then it can be disappointing, but other researchers will be very willing to respond.

Networking, scholarship and communication

The activity of 'networking' has sometimes had a rather tarnished image. For some, it is too associated with attempts to create an impression, perhaps as part of touting for jobs, gaining an outlet for publication, seeking to influence, and so on. But 'networking' should not be too readily dismissed. There should be ethical practices in guiding academic relations, but it should not be forgotten that, broadly, disciplines are built on forms of close communication. As Bendix and Roth (1971: 103) argue:

(Continued)

(Continued)

> As in other disciplines, scholarship in sociology depends on communication concerning the findings and methods of study. In this context every statement made invites consent and helps to define the circle of those who agree, while to some extent marking off those who do not.

Even so, we should not expect relations always to be smooth:

> We are all familiar with the feeling of dismay and anxiety, or with the displays of aggression, when such agreement is not achieved. We are also familiar with the school- or clique-building tendencies that arise from this desire for consensual validation. (Bendix and Roth, 1971: 103)

Bendix and Roth add: 'Like all academic disciplines sociology depends on the existence of a scholarly community. A modern university comprises a congeries of such communities' (Bendix and Roth, 1971: 103).

Contacts can give information that enables a researcher to keep in touch with developments in their area – latest reports, ongoing studies, new methodological practices or techniques, and the existence of relevant groups or centres. Links with other researchers also provide valuable information on more formal outlets for research dissemination, such as journals, edited books planned or forthcoming conferences, research committees in professional associations, and so on. Networking, if defined as contacts with others in the same field for the purpose of discussion on areas of common interest, is not only an essential part of open, useful, stimulating communication but is also the basis of collegiality and often long-term friendship.

The search for funds

The search for funding can be a time-consuming and generally wearying process. Often there is much pressure to gain funding, especially if the researcher is coming to the end of a current research grant, and will soon need further funding to pay the mortgage and weekly bills! Also, there is rising pressure within universities, at least in the UK, to gain funding and to disseminate and publish research findings. Academic promotion and appointments may well depend on research activity, with questions like 'How much research money have you brought into the department?' and 'How many recent publications do you have?' asked of the applicant.

A research grant application may well be in response to a call for proposals by a local or national funding body which wishes for a certain subject area to be researched and which is willing to receive submissions for a small or large grant. Application forms are usually several pages in length and require a detailed outline of the nature and aims of the research, extensive information on costing, and referees who can be contacted. Help for the researcher in filling in the application is variable between academic institutions; advice (on style, organisation, financial detail, and so on) from colleagues who have been successful is often very useful.

The search for funds

The choice of a research area and the possible success in gaining funds is, in part, guided by the current practices of the 'disciplinary and funding community' and how an assessment is made of the importance of a topic and the 'standing' of the theoretical and methodological approaches to be employed.

- An area of study may or may not be 'in fashion'; subject areas rise and fall in research 'popularity'. So, a topic or issue or group may no longer be seen as important as it once was, or of pressing theoretical concern and methodological interest.
- It is apparent that methods and theories emerge or re-emerge and develop 'a following' as they are taken up by leading writers, and in established or new journals, book series, academic groupings and conferences.
- There are the imperatives of public policy which affect sponsoring organisations that may be placing funds for research on some areas, issues and groups according to public or government concerns. A research area or type of research may not attract funds, since other, 'high-profile' areas are considered more 'worthy' of attention.

To work hard on a piece of research and be committed to exploring a set of issues but to experience difficulties in finding funding can be frustrating. It is a knock also to self-esteem, and it may feel at times that personal enthusiasm and energy may have been misplaced if it appears your area is not seen as important. Of course, all researchers, no doubt, feel that their area is central to the discipline and perhaps in some wider societal terms! However, there are heartening stories of researchers whose field was neglected of funds until it suddenly rose to prominence due to media and government attention, and was recognised as a topical and important area.

The research proposal

What is sometimes overlooked in guides to research practice for quantitative and qualitative methods is the potentially long period in which a proposal is considered and prepared. For example, a less experienced researcher or a PhD student researcher, may well have to take several months formulating a research proposal. As Leonard advises:

If you work in the humanities and social sciences … you will spend a lot of time initially defining and refining your topic, deciding the appropriate methodology to use, finding sources and doing fieldwork on your own. You may feel even more isolated and unsupported, culture shocked and in limbo (though this is changing). Even your supervisor's interests may soon be substantially different from your own, despite it initially looking as if you have a lot in common. Little is organized for you outside the taught courses in the first year. There is no timetable, no set reading, and little feedback unless you seek it. Academic interaction in seminars and conferences can be competitive and down-putting, especially if you lack middle class heterosexual confidence. (Leonard, 2001: 63)

For the experienced researcher, a proposed piece of research may have a 'long history' deriving from his or her established research interests and previous studies as well as more recent developments in the field. But, the proposal still has to be 'shaped' to meet funding criteria. Although funding bodies often give tight deadlines, they do usually provide much background information on a particular research 'initiative' in their call for proposals, including lengthy guidelines and detailed forms which have to be completed. As with PhD proposals, internal university procedures will have to be met for approval, including scrutiny by ethics committees (and in relation to health research, external ethical approval) (see Punch, 2000).

Inevitably, compiling the details for the research proposal and making it fit the funding guidelines needs a great deal of energy. Meanwhile, this often has to be done while engaged in other research and/or teaching commitments. The document will have to be checked against the guidelines for applicants, costings and references scrutinised, and a final proofreading accomplished. Then there is the wait for the response from the funding body with a further delay if the proposal is shortlisted. Detailed feedback is usually now given by research bodies, which may include the comments of several referees (on areas such as 'originality', 'value for money' and 'communication plans'). Failing to gain a grant after such an effort can be quite a personal blow. As the applicant, you may not agree with all the comments, but generally you will probably see areas where the application could have been strengthened. It may well be that what you have offered is a topic or approach that, on reflection, is not quite as central as you thought to those required in the call for research applications. You may well have good support from your department, a very interesting topic and are very committed to the research, but you have written what you wish to research rather than fitting the wishes of the funding body. Constructing research proposals is something of an 'art' and success depends upon the skill in meeting the criteria laid out. Evidence of past success in obtaining funding and completing research by you or the team, especially for large grants, can be a factor in receiving further monies.

The experience of qualitative and quantitative research

The 'experiential' aspects of research do not only occur in qualitative studies – the researcher has a life and feelings, and interacts with others when also engaged in more quantitative research! This is not to deny differences between methods and methodological practice. For example, Bryman (1988) makes a useful set of distinctions between 'quantity' and 'quality' in social research, which has a bearing on the research experience. He gives a number of key differences between quantitative and qualitative research traditions, including: the role of researcher can be 'preparatory' or a means to explore the interpretations of actors; the relation between the researcher and research is different in terms of closeness; the researcher is either an 'outsider' or 'insider' in relation to the researched, and 'social reality' is conceived as 'static and imposed or socially constructed by individuals' (Bryman, 1988: 93–104). However, we can add that these differences can be seen as more overlapping in practice than simply 'polar', and, of course, often a research project employs a range of research methods.

Questions concerning research relations in 'quantitative' methods arose in my research in a Welsh valley that used a survey alongside other techniques. A mail questionnaire was sent out with a covering letter and free post reply envelope. Questions were asked on personal background (occupation, income, length of residence) and open questions on 'outlook' on the valley's future. The response rate was much better than expected and only a few replies were poorly completed, so I felt some relief that an initial hurdle had been overcome. Unfortunately, in at least one case the addressee had died and a near relative kindly informed me of the fact. I felt grateful for local people taking the time to fill in the questionnaire, and felt some responsibility to them to 'do my best' with the material. I became more aware of their possible expectations of the research in filling in responses. Pressure of time to overcome the next hurdles – the collation and analysis of the materials, and how it related to previous findings – soon began to bear down on my thoughts.

Innovation in research

For those who have undertaken successfully qualitative or quantitative research previously there is the confidence that comes with repetition, of having tried or considered alternatives before, of knowing more about comparable research and similar procedures. There is also likely to be a supportive network of colleagues of equal standing whose expertise can be drawn on and who have been part of ongoing discussions and exchanges of experiences for a number of years. Of course, the acquisition of experience and 'competence' in ways of conducting research can have its drawbacks. A degree of inflexibility may result by believing that there is simply a 'tried and tested' and 'only' way of doing things, and by being less open to innovation in new methodological or theoretical approaches. There can be an underlying feeling of unease when alternative procedures are offered. The researcher may have pioneered a procedure or at least have some personal commitment to it. Now it may be considered out of date or its basis questioned where it was once seen as 'cutting edge'. The experienced researcher may feel uncomfortable branching into a new procedure or area of study that is unfamiliar and in which competence and standing has to be re-established. Instead of being excited by something new, it may be 'galling' to have a new procedure or analytical slant offered by someone who is deemed a relative newcomer. Of course, such feelings should not arise, but the research environment is as competitive as any other occupational ladder. For the less experienced researcher and postgraduate, there is a possible difficulty where new innovations in methods or techniques may be resisted or doubted by established researchers, including research supervisors.

Research relations in different social settings

There are innumerable research settings and a wide variation in research relations. The research participants may be in 'closed' or 'open settings' according to the degree to which they can move from place to place and make 'life choices'. For example, the study of prisoners brings particular difficulties for research practice and relations, as Cohen and Taylor found in their work on maximum security prisoners:

While there might be certain identifications between us and the prisoners, there are also many areas of disjunction. It was initially not very easy, for example, to feel relaxed in a room which contained a number of supposedly dangerous and volatile criminals. We were rarely conscious of any danger – although the prisoners correctly sensed that one of our colleagues was so nervous during the lecture period that he failed to appear for his subsequent classes. As one member remarked, 'How does it feel teaching people you've read so much about?' (Cohen and Taylor, 1972: 33; see also Cohen and Taylor, 1978)

Expectations of the researcher

Contacts in research (interviewees, informants) can put the 'researcher' into several roles or categories. As an interviewee, people have some general knowledge about 'research' from television or personal experience (e.g. street interviews) which may help or hinder a study. They may have certain expectations of the researcher as an 'academic', as an 'intellectual', as a 'teacher', or as a 'writer-reporter', as someone taking their view to form part of book, article or report. Any of these forms may lead to some particular shaping, perhaps by a caution in individual's responses. Other individuals may relish the chance to be 'consulted' and may be excited by the fact that they are making a (published) contribution. In a related way, there are various common conceptions of what 'research' is and its purpose and use. The researcher has to feel confident in the roles adopted and perceived by others, and reassured that they reflect what is intended as part of the research.

There are certain expectations by researchers and others regarding the appropriate feelings to hold towards particular kinds of research participant and setting. Also, while the researcher brings unique experience and personality, and differing gender, class, sexual and other aspects of social background (see Yow, 2005: Chapter 6), the way the researcher is treated by those in the research context varies according to certain assumptions and perceptions. Easterday et al. (1982) drew attention to the 'specific problems of being a female field researcher in relation to general methodological issues, such as the establishment and maintenance of rapport and research relationships' (Easterday et al., 1982: 62). They record their reflections on a very broad range of their studies, including in 'an art museum, an embalming school, a funeral parlour, a medical team in a nursing home, a military photography programme, a morgue, a newspaper, two social service agencies, a stock brokerage office, a television station and a university film-making programme'. From these studies, they construct a 'typology of sex roles and power', including the 'Fraternity', 'Hustling', the 'Go-fer', the 'Mascot' and the 'Father–Daughter' type (Easterday et al., 1982: 62–5). For example: 'One of the problems a young single female researcher has to deal with is "hustling". Particularly in male-dominated settings where the observer is talking to one male at a time ... the male–female games come early to the fore' (Easterday et al., 1982: 64). Another type is the 'Go-fer', which is found where the female researcher may be expected to take the role of 'go-fer' – fetching this or that as in clerical errands assumed 'a typical role for the woman, to which men can easily relate'.

Of further interest is the 'Father–Daughter' type of research relationship which combines age, gender and power:

Older males in a setting may interact with a young female researcher in a manner we describe as paternalistic. Given the legitimacy of traditional sex role relationships, the father–daughter relationship offers older males – threatened by young women or unable to interact with young women as peers – a safe, predefined interactional context. (Easterday et al., 1982: 65)

The lesson to draw from Easterday et al.'s typology is to be aware of the role expectations that may result from your status, gender and other social dimensions (see Brewer, 2000: 99–101). In addition, the investigator needs to be cognisant of the negotiations and challenges that may be necessary to carry out the work without feeling compromised, uncomfortable or bullied. Researchers need to make clear their own position and intent in the research role, while also being aware of the expectations of the research group and an organisation's policies on staff relations.

Competing research roles

The researcher in organisations

A feature of research may well be how an organisation fits the researcher into its existing pattern of relationships or roles. The researcher may find him or herself moving or caught between the role(s) given or expected by the organisation and those of a researcher, while also trying to fit in and gain knowledge of the organisational routines and personnel. For example, Hey undertook a 'small-scale participant observation study conducted in two city schools in the mid-late 1980s'. She researched in a 'large mixed comprehensive in a middle-class suburb' and a smaller comprehensive within a mainly working-class area nearby. She says that aside from her 'inexperience in conducting research', her 'field relations' 'were also complicated by other factors: the circumstances of the school, the nature of the project (privileging girls) as well as by the choice of fieldwork methods (participant observation)'. As she quotes from early fieldnotes:

Felt foolish 'cos I couldn't recollect the names of all the staff with whom I'd just been liaising. I kept calling Mrs. Harris, Mrs Taylor, *felt just like a new girl*, overwhelmed by the bureaucratic nightmares that schools are (to newcomers). Not only do you have to remember the [layout of] buildings but also: staff names; statuses; subjects; timetables; timings; routines; protocols and facilities. (Hey, 2002: 68–9)

The researcher can be engaged in a number of 'competing' roles during the course of research – student, fund-raiser, author, 'confidant' or disseminator – which may create some tensions or 'role-strain'. For some researchers the overlap between 'formal' and 'informal' roles in research may be intentional, as in feminist and some other research, where the participant is conceived as less of an 'informant', 'respondent' or 'subject' and more as a collaborator, friend or helper in the research. But, 'competing' or 'multiple' roles can lead to certain problems. For instance, an important difficulty can arise between the investigator as a researcher and as a practitioner. Moch relates her concerns around being a researcher and also a nurse:

> My experience as a researcher in qualitative research has been a source of great reflection, inner struggle, and ethical questioning. Some of the difficulty occurred because of my being a nurse as well as a researcher. At times, I wondered if I was first a nurse and then a researcher, or first a researcher and then a nurse. Sometimes, the difficulty arose because of my experience as a mother, wife, midlife woman, or professor. In other words, the researcher experience and all the reflection and struggle happened, in part, because of who I am. And I don't want to change that. (Moch, 2000a: 7)

Moch's research reveals the difficulties of being in two roles – a researcher and practitioner – to such an extent that the two meld together as equal partners as 'researcher-practitioner' (Moch, 2000a: 9). Similar 'blurring' of roles occurs more frequently in research than is perhaps realised. Some important issues can arise. For example, does the researcher give information which might help, for instance, the health of the researched? If so, how and when is this done? How are the shifts in role possible, justifiable and understandable to the 'researched patient'? Valerie Yow, an oral historian, adds a further note of caution regarding 'role confusion' in relation to interviewing. We expect to 'get on' with our interviewees, share some similar assumptions and for the interview to be a 'success', but in her view:

> The interviewer must keep in mind that a professional relationship is not a friendship and make that clear, if need be, to the narrator. When the interviewer has a negative reaction to what the narrator is saying or is distracted by some interpersonal chemistry, he or she must consciously keep in mind the purpose of the interview. (Yow, 2005: 179)

In my own community research, I made friends with a number of 'interviewees', exchanging Christmas cards, making phone calls to see how they were, and so on, as well as asking for 'news of the valley'. I often found during the research that I was in various roles at different times, or even in simultaneous roles: as researcher seeking information, as an interested historian with a concern for the locality and its social issues, as a friend exchanging experiences of family and other relationships, or as a confidant being told of 'local gossip'. Other perhaps more formal or distant roles emerged: as guest in a house or club, as a visiting speaker to a regular group meeting, as a paying guest in a bed and breakfast establishment, as a party member sharing the same political commitments, as an academic discussing the area with other academics (sometimes in the research context itself), among others. The 'self-examination' of my research roles was not debilitating. I began to gain a confidence in my own research abilities, in the purpose of the research, and feel a sense of achievement – while under severe time constraints and outside pressures.

Key points to remember on researcher experience: the researcher's role

Discussions on the role of the researcher have until recently neglected the 'inner' or 'emotional' aspects of 'researcher experience':

- The researcher's role is a complex, multifaceted one, which can contain various tensions (e.g. between researcher and practitioner, or researcher as 'data gatherer' and as a 'friend').
- The researcher's own life is involved in the research process and affects the experience of research.
- The researcher may place – some say should place – him or herself directly in the research rather than portray themselves as someone neutral or detached.
- The researcher will be involved in a range of different relationships during the course of research, with those researched, collaborators and colleagues, funders, research audience and non-research associations.
- To be identified as a 'researcher' can be important for individual identity, academic or social status, and self-respect.

Summary

There are many different styles and types of research project that may comprise a mixture of quantitative and qualitative work. The conduct of research involves the investigator's life, including a 'personal' investment. Different styles or types of research and research topic have a differing status depending on the current concerns of the discipline and the 'fashion' for certain subjects and issues, which may well reflect wider social priorities. Networking can give important support to the researcher, for example, in providing guidance, encouragement and personal support as well as an outlet to 'sound out' ideas.

Further reading

There are a number of collections of personal accounts of sociological research work and careers, often by leading sociologists. For the 'classic' account, see P.E. Hammond (ed.) (1964) *Sociologists at Work: Essays on the Craft of Social Research* (London: Basic Books). Also very interesting for research practice and careers are: C. Bell and S. Encel (eds) (1978) *Inside the Whale: Ten Personal Accounts of Social Research* (Oxford: Pergamon Press); I.L. Horowitz (ed.) (1970) *Sociological Self Images: A Collective Portrait* (Oxford: Pergamon Press); M.W. Riley (ed.) (1988) *Sociological Lives* (London: Sage); and N. Hallowell et al. (eds) (2005) *Reflections on Research* (Maidenhead: Open University Press). For discussions of the researcher's own biography and involvement in relations with the researched, see *Sociology* (journal) (1993) Special Issue: 'Biography and Autobiography in Sociology', 27 (1). In searching for funds the websites of major funding bodies give detailed advice on new project areas and how to apply (including proposal forms and how they should be completed), for example, for the Economic and Social Research Council (UK) see http://esrcsocietytoday. ac.uk.

3

THE 'EMOTIONAL' ASPECTS OF RESEARCH

Field researchers learn – through their teachers, texts, and colleagues – how to feel, think, and act. As members of the larger discipline, fieldworkers share a culture dominated by the ideology of professionalism or, more specifically, the ideology of science. According to that ideology, emotions are suspect. They contaminate research by impeding objectivity, hence they should be removed. (Kleinman and Copp, 1993: 2)

If informants are people and have rights that affect ethical practice, ethnographers are also human and have identities that affect research practice. (Brewer, 2000: 99)

Roles carry with them both certain actions and the emotions and attitudes that belong to these actions. The professor putting on an act that pretends to wisdom comes to feel wise. (Berger, 1966: 113)

Research and 'emotional labour'

The 'personal side' of research tends to be given rather limited and patchy attention in traditional textbooks, where it is commonly subsumed under difficulties in 'entering the field' or perhaps an aspect of the interview situation or concerns with 'researcher bias'. What is broadly missing in such accounts of research practice are the 'emotional' and 'experiential' aspects of research or the day-to-day feelings which are experienced in the conduct of all types of research. 'Feelings' or 'moods' are very much part of the experience of research and relations – they are as inescapable, as in other areas of the investigator's life (see Hochschild, 1983).

> Although there is no doubt that people often act reasonably and are capable of rational decision-making, they never do so in the complete absence of emotion. Even what may seem purely practical tasks are generally replete with emotional freight. Routine chores like mowing the lawn or washing dishes are performed under the direct influence of prevailing moods, attitudes and feelings. Onerous tasks are typically tackled in ways that express boredom, enthusiasm or irritability. (Layder, 2004: 25)

Research is an emotional experience. 'Emotionality'

> … is present in the moods and feelings individuals bring to a study. It is present in the lives of those who are studied. It is present in the interactions that go on between researchers and subjects. It is present in the observations that are gathered. It is part of power and of being powerful, or powerless. (Denzin, 2001: 50)

Personal elements in research can take many forms, ranging widely in their origin and nature, from guilt and fear, to delight and euphoria, and all feelings in between! Some of the emotions apparent during research may be due to pressures from a researcher's institution or funders to complete the research. A researcher may have a forthcoming deadline for a written report or a chapter of a dissertation due for a supervisor's comments. Personal pressures to complete the research, and perhaps to begin another piece of research, or to move on in a career by taking up another post can be important concerns at the back of the researcher's mind. Outside anxieties unrelated to the research may also compete with the emotional and physical demands of the study.

Research and mental and physical demands

Research makes a number of demands on the capacities of a researcher which can vary over time – fieldwork, conducting a survey, interviewing, or searching documents all produce personal challenges. Hey (2002) reports that her research on a group of school children put her to numerous mental and physical tests as she followed the routine school life of a group of girls:

(Continued)

(Continued)

In the course of the fieldwork I played rounders; went on cross-country runs; attended registration/pastoral time; stood around on fields at play-time; ate in the cafeteria; sat in on swathes of lessons; occasionally visited the staffroom; went to school plays and end of term demob ceremonies and leavers' assemblies. Rushing around covering the official as well as the more illicit girls' activities demanded, at 35, a certain stamina as well as a willing suspension of disbelief on the part of both the girls and myself. (Hey, 2002: 74)

Research work, especially where it requires direct contact with 'informants', 'respondents', or 'subjects', can be likened to 'emotional labour' (Hochschild, 1983) – as in relations between the social worker and client, the nurse and patient, although each occupational area has its own particular type.

… Hochschild's idea that many jobs require emotion work normally found in informal settings, suggests that rather than driving out genuine intimacy altogether, 'the system' in the guise of the company, transmutes and co-opts such life-world elements for its own ends. The real issue is how much, and what type of emotional labour is required in particular jobs and how much sincerity and real feelings are impinged upon, or damaged as a result. (Layder, 2004: 75)

The 'emotional labour' invested in such relations has a legacy – we continue thinking and feeling 'emotionally' about these relations in other social settings and sometimes for a very long time after they have taken place.

'Reflexivity' and the research experience

'Reflexivity' in research has become a common theme in methodological discussion but it can mean several different things. In one meaning it can merely be the necessary mundane description and consideration on the method chosen, the research actions taken and some justification of the choices made. Reflexivity, rather more, is a conscious 'critical reflection on your own presence in your text, [an] admission of problems and [an] awareness that a process of persuasion is underway' (Ramazanoğlu, 2002: 163). It can therefore take the form of a rigorous 'assessment' of the research experience and process, of what 'worked' in terms of procedure or interpretation, as well as 'intimate' revelations of inner thoughts and feelings. Where the latter involves relations with informants and colleagues, or effects of research commitments on outside relations, there are ethical considerations of confidentiality and potential harm to those involved. 'Reflexivity' has a direct bearing on how the researcher's role is understood. 'Experience' now becomes something that is a 'resource' rather than a hindrance or source of bias which is to be recognised, 'interrogated', and reflected upon as part of the research practice. In taking into account the life of the researcher in sociological practice, the traditional notion of the researcher as a 'technicist', 'observer' and 'recorder' of situations is being challenged (Brewer, 2000: 126–33).

Feminist research, 'reflexivity' and 'personal experience'

In feminist research 'personal experience' can be the very starting point of a study, the material from which the researcher develops questions:

> Feminist researchers use the strategy of 'starting from one's own experi-
> ence' for many purposes. It defines our research questions, leads us to
> sources of useful data, gains the trust of others in doing the research, and
> enables us to partially test our findings. Feminist researchers frequently
> start with an issue that bothers them personally and then use everything
> they can get hold of to study it. (Reinharz, 1992: 259)

According to Reinharz, feminist research is 'frequently a blend of an intellectual question and a personal trouble' (Reinharz, 1992: 260). The 'emotional' side of research, instead of being ruled out as a threat to detachment and objectivity in research practice, can be considered reflexively as aiding research practice. While there are quite a number of 'feminist perspectives' (see Freedman, 2001) and sometimes sharp theoretical and methodological disagreement, for example in the use of qualitative and quantitative methods, there is a commonality in seeking to relate the experience of women with a recognition of the feminist researcher's role in a 'reflexive' practice.

Everyday life skills in research

A range of 'everyday life skills' are required in research. For example, Blaxter et al. give reading, listening, watching, choosing, questioning, summarizing, organizing, writing, reflecting and presenting (Blaxter et al., 2001: 55–8). These 'ordinary' skills will usually need some refinement for the purpose of research. For example, the researcher needs to develop the 'art of listening':

Everything that human beings are or do, no matter how common-place, can become significant for sociological research. Another such peculiar value is inherent in the sociologist's necessity to listen to others without volunteering his [*sic*] own views. The art of listening, quietly and with full attention, is something that any sociologist must acquire if he is to engage in empirical studies. (Berger, 1966: 188)

In this view, the skills we use in our daily lives provide a 'ready route' into how we consider methodological procedures. Thus, how we utilise and consider everyday skills has relevance for how we construct and practise research. This point can also be extended by a more detailed examination of 'feeling skills' or how we 'manage' our emotions in daily living and, further, in the formulation, conduct and experience of research.

Everyday emotional skills in research

The list below is not meant to be 'exhaustive' but seeks to show the range of 'emotional skills' that it may be necessary to employ during a study. They range from 'interpersonal skills' to more 'self-assessment skills'. The employment of these skills will depend on the researcher's experience of a particular situation and the type of research:

- Understanding
- Empathy
- Reflection
- Tact
- Integrity
- Negotiation
- Sense of self
- Perspective
- Commitment

In my research I have routinely considered my use of these skills. By such reflection, the researcher realises the extent to which he or she can draw on and develop emotional skills, for example, in meeting new people in new situations.

Experiential distraction

There are instances in a study when we can become distracted. Situations can arise that may take us away from the main task. However, we may also seek out distractions from a current activity that has become laborious (e.g.

transcribing research interviews, writing notes from background reading, routine filing, and so on). Some such distractions can be a welcome break but can potentially interfere with the completion of the research task in hand. Doing some more 'routine' activity, although not as potentially exciting, may be a way of putting off something more 'challenging'. However, it may also enable a re-concentration and renewal of effort, for example, in the detailed organisation and interpretation of material – sometimes 'ordinary' tasks have a kind of therapeutic effect. Even so, often it may be easier to do the next routine data collection rather than doing anything more challenging with material already gathered. Of course, certain tasks are just rather tiresome but necessary, and should not be rushed.

Time management and 'personal control'

Many of the pressures of research are related to time, whether it is in the routine collecting and analysing of data in quantitative research, the complications involved in arranging and conducting forms of interview, the all-consuming days and months of fieldwork, or the intricacies of managing a research grant or filling in expense forms. There will be days or periods, despite how hard you work, when the research will seem to stretch away – as the next task, it is feared, will be delayed, setting back the day when the research findings are complete and the final document is delivered. No matter how well organised and how efficient you are, some anxiety regarding the passage of time will arise.

The key principles of time management for a researcher are:

- Organise! Organise!
- Set realistic, short-term (daily, weekly, monthly) targets.
- Keep an eye on longer-term deadlines.
- Review the research timetable, discuss progress with others and seek advice early, especially when you have doubts about meeting major deadlines.

The 'management' of activities should not become an obsession, for example planning every small activity for every minute of the day. Rather, it should be a flexible guide that will inspire confidence and a feeling of competence, and thereby a sense of 'personal control'.

- Use a 'time schedule diary' to note tasks and time spent on them per day or week.
- By timing tasks, future activities can be planned more carefully.

(Continued)

(Continued)

- Do one activity at a time – do not attempt to do all those pending activities at once!
- While doing a job, if something comes to mind, note it and file it for later attention.
- Some distraction is good, it can be useful as a relief.
- Too much distraction and time is wasted.
- Measure and plan research time so that a home–research balance can be reached, leaving time to oneself for leisure and relaxation.
- Inevitably there will be times when things go well, when tasks are completed satisfactorily and quickly. At other times, progress seems slow – but do not despair!
- Time organisation shows more clearly what has been achieved and what is to be done. (See Cryer, 2000; 117–31.)

Motivation in research

A researcher or a PhD student may become driven by a feeling that time should not be wasted. Sometimes feelings of inadequacy and futility are to be expected, as though the effort expended does not result in the ready outcomes. New researchers may question their commitment to a research career, or broader academic career, especially when low pay (in the UK) and the uncertainty of the next grant is taken into account. The increasing demands to have a PhD, to publish, to present conference papers, and to gain teaching experience to start an academic career all present pressures that 'test' research commitment.

Motivational doubts

When having doubts about motivation to carry on an investigation, researchers should ask themselves a number of questions (see Blaxter et al., 2001: 9–11):

- Why did I begin the research?
- What was intended by the research?
- What have I achieved so far in terms of completing the research?
- What 'skills' have I developed?
- What do I wish to achieve by the research – for myself, for the subject area, for the group researched, or the wider society?
- What I have learnt about myself?

Of course, the researcher may find on closer examination that he or she is not as motivated as previously thought. Research commonly involves a high level of motivation – certainly for a postgraduate research degree. If the motivation is lacking, then either some has to be 'found' or a decision has to be made about future research involvement.

Renewing motivation

There are a number of ways in which motivation can be renewed:

- By a 'realistic' review of research progress. Discuss with others (e.g. supervisor, collaborator) what has been achieved and any future plans.
- By considering a shift in direction or emphasis of the research – a lack of motivation may be due to the fact that research difficulties are arising because some aspect of the research is not feasible.
- By placing the research in the context of personal development – the skills or expertise that have been obtained and that can be 'transferred'.
- By seeking out those who will be interested in your research and may be a source of encouragement.
- By reviewing the relative demands on your time and resources made by your research and non-research activities.
- By keeping in mind the objective of the research. Remember – although there is a deadline the completion of your research will be a personal achievement (see Blaxter et al., 2001: 12).

Working with others in research

A team of researchers, some of whom are more senior than others, commonly conducts large-scale research. Relationships within a team, both formally and informally, may be very varied. It is obviously important for the conduct and success of a research project that tasks and roles are clear and that personal relationships have a positive, practical basis. Questions of the researcher's relations with the group and its members will arise as well as his or her particular role within the group (see Blaxter et al., 2001: 137–45; Platt, 1976: Chapter 7).

> Being able to work with particular colleagues, and trusting and accepting the authority of seniors, is often dependent on whether the individual feels 'psychologically embraced' by the company in terms of deserved career rewards ... the quality of an individual's bond with an employing organization is revealed in how 'significant' he or she feels (in terms of their value and contribution) to that organization. It is hard for an employee not to measure 'significance' or personal value as reflected in their achievement of career rewards. (Layder, 2004: 76)

The researcher may be an inexperienced member of a group or a PhD student with a supervisory team to guide him or her. But, personal difficulties associated with research can be dealt with

… by recognizing that one has been put (back) into an apprentice position, and coping with this through negotiating a more equal relationship with one's supervisor; and by establishing solidarities with others in the same situation, rather than by retreating into one's room and adjusting one's head. (Leonard, 2001: 171)

Guidance from a team leader or supervisor will vary, not only according to the stage of the research, but also due to the personalities involved, the level of the 'apprentice's' experience and other factors. The rapport between leader/supervisor and the new researcher will also differ. It is worth remembering that the research leader or supervisor is also under 'some pressure' since he or she will want the research group's work or the PhD to be successful. A dissertation may, in fact, be drawn from a research project which involves the supervisor.

Relations between researchers

It is generally assumed that relations between researchers are usually without tension. However, within research teams engaged in all types of social investigation differences will emerge at times, and relationships between individuals will undergo some pressure. We do not usually read about the 'inside' story of how a study progressed, and even less so (for obvious reasons) of the personal relationships involved. Of interest here is Bell's (1977) account of the strain within a community study research team and their families:

All three families bought houses in the town – in itself a fairly extraordinary thing to do for what was known in advance to be a fairly limited stay. … Strains – Fieldwork bears heavily on the families of those who do it. I must emphasise again that we were all living there with our families – I, for instance, participant observed as an expectant father in the maternity wing of Banbury's hospital. We shopped, used pubs, and went to parties, movies and so on as ordinary, if hyperactive, inhabitants. The *structural* strain of fieldwork between fieldworker as friend and fieldworker as stranger resulted in great *personal* strain. We lived with this for two years at considerable strain. (Bell, 1977: 50, 59; see also Newby, 1977: 63–6)

This is an instance of the researcher's 'research life' being very much embedded in his 'outside' life – in the family and surrounding community – and the difficulties that can result for the research team (and their families).

'Collaboration' in research also includes the relations with 'respondents'. The expectation of 'closeness' to respondents or 'subjects' varies according to the method employed. For some commentators, fieldworkers should experience aspects of research, such as a degree of the pain, suffering or elation of the researched in their lives. More mundanely, in fact, some shared experience is hard to avoid if the researcher is spending days, even weeks or months within, perhaps, a remote cultural setting. Rather than ignoring or trying to separate off our emotions regarding the conduct of research with others, we should use them positively, and attempt to understand and acknowledge them and the decisions they influence. As Tedlock states, in relation to ethnography, research involves moral choices: 'Because ethnography is both a process and a product, ethnographers' lives are embedded within their field experiences in such a way that all of their interactions involve moral choices' (Tedlock, 2000: 455).

Of course, research of various kinds carries some moral choices in relation to the respondents, even if the method chosen is not predicated on 'closeness' and 'continuous' contact. These can include, for instance, the kinds of question asked (or not asked), types of consent sought, the uses and benefits of the research in relation to the respondent and possible adverse consequences despite efforts to meet the principle of 'not to cause harm'. There is a related issue of the response of the researcher to what he or she is being told by respondents or informants during research and the feelings that this can generate. The researcher may feel disgusted, upset or angry by what is said on a particular issue or about another group – we usually expect to 'get along' with respondents and share the same values and outlook instead of being 'uncomfortable' in a situation (see Kleinman and Copp, 1993: 28, 33).

Subjective support

It is often the ties with colleagues engaged in a similar research project elsewhere or a wider body of colleagues and contacts that can give very important intellectual, practical or emotional support. Equally important is that relationships between investigators and their partners, family, friends or others are supportive and nurtured. These non-academic ties can give invaluable help and advice, even by merely listening to the researcher's account of daily activities. Non-academic relationships are essential so that we can share our work–life anxieties, achievements and personal development. They also provide emotional 'resources' to bolster confidence in showing interest and giving encouragement. Emotional support from a wider circle of colleagues, and the personal circle of attachments, are not sufficiently noted in research texts as important foundations for an enriching research 'life'. Such wider supports provide 'emotional safety valves' and 'safety nets', and help 'emotional recuperation'; they serve to maintain a sense of self-esteem, and are a source of reassurance that the research is worthwhile. We all like to know that we are doing something that has some benefit, that we have skills and competences, and that we are not simply wasting our time and others' time, money, and effort. In short, 'subjective support' in research is very important for the overall well-being of the researcher and the success of the project or dissertation. Leonard gives practical suggestions (for female postgraduates) for 'building support for yourself' (Leonard, 2001: 161). She says that within the university:

Women often feel isolated and alienated by a 'chilly climate' in their own departments, so it is doubly important for us to build up support in and outside the university. This also helps to reduce making unreasonable demands on your supervisor ... (Leonard, 2001: 162)

She argues that there is often less attention paid to what women say. When they talk they are interrupted whereas points made by men are taken on board. She adds that it should not be assumed that universities are devoid of the sexist behaviour and discriminatory practices found elsewhere (Leonard, 2001: 161).

Overcoming isolation

Doing a postgraduate research degree and in research more generally, if you are the main or single researcher, can be a lonely experience. Your postgraduate supervisors will be busy doing other things apart from seeing you. Even though meetings with your supervisory team may be on a regular basis, you may not see its members a great deal other than at arranged times. Living alone, perhaps separated from family and friends, finding yourself eating on your own, engaged in leisure alone, lacking others to talk to, and so on can be very difficult circumstances to cope with. 'Isolation' can lead to an irregular organisation of your day and may affect your physical and mental health. So, it is essential to establish social contacts.

Institutional contacts

- Seek out other postgraduates and other researchers with similar interests in the university.
- Seek out researchers at other institutions in the same field.
- Form a group to discuss ideas and research in a constructive, helpful and critical manner.
- Get to know others in the department not involved in your research but who may also be supportive.
- Make good connections with departmental, library and other support staff.
- Make use of the facilities of the university graduate centre and take part in its activities. (See Leonard, 2001: 162–6.)

Social activities and living normally

- Get to know people – join a club at the university.
- If single, consider going into shared university or other accommodation.

Pattern of life

- Discuss problems of workload with those in and outside the project, especially if the research time is unduly impinging on your private life. Workload demands should be clear and not excessive. You may need to identify tasks formerly unstated or unnecessary tasks or demands.
- Inexperienced researchers often seek 'perfection', making 'extra' efforts and perhaps failing to distinguish sufficiently between what are essential and what are secondary activities.
- Be clear about what you can change and what you cannot – and seek guidance.
- Try to keep a regular, 'normal' work pattern (depending on the stage or kind of research undertaken), leaving time for outside activities and obligations.

Dealing with anxiety and stress

The issue of anxiety or stress in academic life has received a great deal of prominence recently. Academic and research organisations should have policies and procedures to meet the issue of stress among employees, and sometimes associated problems such as harassment or bullying. A research team should also have a clear basis and means of allocating tasks and provide appropriate supervision and support that takes account of the capabilities of the new researcher. Stress can be caused by a wide range of factors, including excessive demands of tasks and time leading to overwork, feeling undervalued for your efforts, unnecessary administration, and difficulties with colleagues and superiors. A lack of consultation or input into decisions, an uncertain job future, frequent organisational changes, performance goals set too high, shifts in procedure, inadequate pay and limited promotion possibilities, and a lack of support from colleagues are also factors (see Cryer, 2000: 222).

Dealing with emotions in research

Research brings with it a variety of shifting emotions towards informants, co-workers, researchers engaged in the same field, other colleagues in the organisation, family and friends, sponsors and others. Variations in emotions are to be expected but a 'personal perspective' on the research experience is necessary to avoid the tiring effect of mood swings.

(Continued)

(Continued)

Combating anxieties

Research can damage your physical and mental well-being; it can become an obsession, dominating your thoughts and your interaction with important others outside the work setting. All research tends to have difficult moments. There may be, at times, negative feelings regarding the informants or even towards other colleagues engaged in the research. The possible negative effects of doing research can be minimised in the following ways:

- 'Pace yourself' physically and mentally.
- If you feel your health is being affected, then seek appropriate help.
- Ask others engaged in the same type of research or on the same research topic if they have also faced difficulties.
- Balance private and research life demands – recognise that you need company and different activities, that you are not just a researcher but also a friend, a family member, and you have other interests.
- Discuss workload problems with other researchers on the project and/or the postgraduate supervisor – usually these can be resolved quickly.
- Do not expect too much and 'over-push' yourself – you can only do so much! Take advice from others (colleagues, supervisor, co-workers, other students and, if necessary, counsellors) on what is 'manageable'.

Positive feelings

When negative feelings are experienced, a way of gaining some perspective is to think of what has gone well and concentrate on previous moments of satisfaction, invigoration and optimism. Remember past achievements and count the successes that have been reached so far in the research.

Enjoy the points in the research when things are going well – tasks completed, difficulties overcome, 'breakthroughs' made – but, mentally log these positive feelings for future reference as a counterweight if difficulties occur.

In the early days as a new researcher, attendance at seminars (e.g. those given by guest speakers in the department) is a good way of obtaining a 'feel' of the intellectual culture – a particular field, what research is taking place, possible shared concerns, and for making friendships. Without sources of support the swings in commitment and mood during research can be more difficult to bear. For some, the pressures of research can have very detrimental effects on health and lead to anxiety, alcohol abuse, depression and other problems, and a 'vicious circle of less leisure, less exercise, sleeplessness, and lack of concentration, leading to working longer hours' (Leonard, 2001: 170). Leonard rightly adds that there can be 'physical stresses' that are often overlooked, for instance, the 'risks of repetitive strain injury to one's hands and arms, and damage to one's eyes from hours in front of computer screens' (Leonard, 2001: 170).

'Stress' and the practice of research

Stress is frequently mentioned in media discussions of contemporary work and we may often discuss it in broad terms, and perhaps in relation to our own 'troubles' with those closest to us both in and outside the work context. Discussion of stress also features strongly in the academic press. It can be associated with anxiety and depression. Such conditions can build up over a long period; it is not usually a temporary feeling of being down or nervous, but something more unusual and rather deeper.

'Stress', 'anxiety' and 'depression' are often not fully understood and are sometimes dismissed as routine problems of working or an indicator that someone cannot cope with the job. In fact, these conditions are both more common and debilitating than is often perceived. They can be associated with the complex and growing demands of a job coupled with a lack of training and insufficient emotional and other support. Financial pressures, new living arrangements, outside commitments, general tasks and daily problems are extra sources of strain.

Effects of experiencing stress

Kinman and Jones (2004), in 'Working to the limit', give some useful information on stress and academia in UK. They note that stress is officially defined as an 'adverse reaction' to excessive demands and pressure. Around 70 per cent of academic respondents in a large survey reported that they found their job stressful, with a half saying that they could not manage their workload. Nearly all agreed that the pressure to publish had increased significantly in the previous five years, with a large majority saying that pressure to gain funding had also risen. Importantly, more than one-third agreed strongly that work demand had interfered with non-work life (Kinman and Jones, 2004). A recent study for the Association of University Teachers (UK) found that 49 per cent of academics reported levels of stress that needed medical intervention, 62 per cent said they could not cope with their job, while 41 per cent said their main interests were focused on work and 40 per cent did not take all their holiday leave. Academics found it difficult to put the work demands into a broader life perspective (McCall, 2006: 64).

Key points to remember on researcher experience: the 'emotional' aspects of research

- Research is an emotional activity. Emotions or feelings are an integral part of the experience of research.
- Research is a social activity. The researcher participates in a range of social relations within and outside the research process.
- Textbooks can only give a very partial preparation for the personal experiences and effects of research.
- Research draws on both methodological and 'everyday life' skills.
- 'Subjective support' from others engaged in the research, from a wider circle of colleagues and in private relations is vital.
- A degree of anxiety, strain and a lack of motivation at times are a normal part of research – they are faced by all researchers, and can be reduced. Seek social support and, if necessary, more expert advice. Your physical and mental health is more important than research!

Summary

The conduct of research exhibits an 'emotional labour'. Research draws on the 'everyday' practical and emotional 'life skills' that the researcher applies in the routine of daily living and social relationships, for example, in collaborating with and supporting others. 'Subjective support' is a necessary part of the research activity, although the researcher is rarely completely 'alone' (at least, not for long periods). He or she is a 'social being' who needs to communicate, receive and exchange feelings, and have a sense of worth. The opportunity to have a 'social life' outside research – although friendships and conviviality among research colleagues is not unknown! – is essential for the researcher to have an emotional and physical break from his or her endeavours. This is not only important for the inexperienced researcher, but also for those who have undertaken substantial amounts of social investigation. Personal feelings associated with research problems and difficulties are a routine part of investigation, as in other areas of life. But extra support and expert advice should be sought and further help considered if these difficulties begin to cause harmful personal effects. It is important to try to anticipate undue pressures (e.g. unrealistic deadlines and workload set by others or oneself) and seek ways of preventing them.

Further reading

For issues on researcher roles and experience with particular reference to female researchers and postgraduates, see L. Easterday et al. (1982) 'The making of a female researcher: role problems in fieldwork', in R.G. Burgess (ed.),

Field Research: A Sourcebook and Field Manual (London: Unwin Hyman) and D. Leonard (2001) *A Woman's Guide to Doctoral Studies* (Buckingham: Open University Press). Leonard is also very useful for postgraduate experience generally, but see also: P. Cryer (2000) *The Research Student's Guide to Success* (Buckingham: Open University Press); N. Gilbert (ed.) (2006) *The Postgraduate Guidebook* (London: Sage); and D. Wilkinson (2005) *The Essential Guide to Postgraduate Study* (London: Sage). A detailed introduction to 'people skills' and the 'art of reflection' needed by students is given in S. Cottrell (2003) *Skills for Success* (Basingstoke: Palgrave Macmillan). On reflexivity and the self, emotions in fieldwork and interviewing, and understanding emotions in a range of social contexts, see: K. Etherington (2004) *Being a Reflexive Researcher: Using Our Selves in Research* (London: Jessica Kingsley Publishers); N. Hallowell et al. (eds) (2005) *Reflections on Research* (Maidenhead: Open University Press); S. Kleinman and M.A. Copp (1993) *Emotions and Fieldwork* (London: Sage); D. Layder (2004) *Emotion in Social Life* (London: Sage); V.R. Yow (2005) *Recording Oral History: A Guide for the Humanities and Social Sciences* (2nd edn, Walnut Creek, CA: AltaMira Press), Chapter 6; and W.B. Shaffir and R.A. Stebbins (eds) (1991) *Experiencing Fieldwork: An Inside View of Qualitative Research* (London: Sage).

4

ENTERING THE RESEARCH: THE PRESENTATION OF THE RESEARCHER'S SELF

Chapter overview

The researcher's self in research
Sociological imagination and research practice
Early days in research
Entering research contexts
Reasons to research
The PhD experience
Research 'hold-ups'
Key points to remember on researcher experience: entering the research
Summary
Further reading

When an individual plays a part he [sic] implicitly requests his observers to take seriously the impression that is fostered before them. They are asked to believe that the character they see actually possesses the attributes he appears to possess, that the task he performs will have the consequences that are implicitly claimed for it, and that, in general, matters are what they appear to be. (Goffman, 1971: 28)

The researcher's self in research

Much discussion of research practice has centred around the 'first steps' or gaining entrance to the research setting and associated ethical issues on making clear to contacts the nature and purpose of the research. These discussions touch on the researcher as an individual facing a challenge, yet a deeper examination of the researcher's self during the start of research, the inner life and its relation to the context (and other academic and non-academic contexts) have remained largely unexplored until fairly recently. These issues tended to be 'cordoned off' as already 'managed', for example, by the application of the principles of neutrality and objectivity in research conduct. Instead, due to feminist and other influences, the dynamic between the 'presentation' of the researcher self in the study context and wider relations are now quite widely recognised as part of the 'constitution' of the research process. As Denzin says, a 'gendered, historical self is brought to this process. This self, as a set of shifting identities, has its own history with the situated practices that define and shape the public issues and private troubles being studied' (Denzin, 2001: 3).

The experience of the 'researcher's self' in research, as I have argued, can be likened to a 'voyage of discovery', both into self-knowledge as well as into the field chosen. Cohen, an anthropologist, in discussing the researcher's role, calls for a 'self-consciousness' in fieldwork (Cohen, 1992). He concedes that such a concern does not mean that investigation should simply be a reflection by the investigator of his or her own past struggles and current problems; the intention is how to lay bare the relationship between the researcher's self and the conduct of the research.

Researcher behaviour and presentation

Davies, drawing on research in a prison, points out aspects of research relations in a 'constrained' environment that can be applied to other settings. For instance, whether researchers should offer 'inducements' to interviewees who are incarcerated and 'impoverished' (Davies, 2000: 87). Interestingly, she also raises issues of wider relevance for researcher behaviour and presentation, which are not usually found in textbooks on research procedure, but are potentially important for study experience in other contexts:

> Lesser concerns were related to a fear of the unknown: what to wear? What to take with me? Whether I would arrive on time. Whether the prison gate and security had been informed of my arrival and my business. Whether there would be any obstacles to going in and getting on with the interviews. How I would manage to conduct myself appropriately and credibly with both staff and inmates.

Nevertheless, she says that there are contextual differences with other fields:

> Although many worries and concerns are common to both prison- and community-based interviews, some matters are location specific. For example, although gaining access to women in the institutional setting was not entirely free of difficulties, access to women who had offended, or who continued to offend and who (still) had their freedom and liberty, can prove a slower and more cumbersome process of negotiation. (Davies, 2000: 87)

The conduct of all research – as in other areas of life – is a 'performance' or rather a set of performances in which feelings, views and physical well-being are managed and 'impressions' given. For Goffman, the individual has a 'belief in the impression of reliability that he [*sic*] attempts to engender in those among whom he finds himself' (Goffman, 1971: 28). However, if we applied a simple view of the researcher as 'impression manager', he or she could be seen as a 'cynical performer', merely 'conning' the 'audience' (respondents, colleagues, funders) in the study context according to straightforward personal 'self interest' (Goffman, 1971: 29). Even so, any social role, including that of 'researcher', brings with it an exterior 'front':

When an actor takes on an established social role, usually he [*sic*] finds that a particular front has already been established for it. Whether his acquisition of the role was primarily motivated by a desire to perform the given task or by a desire to maintain the corresponding front, the actor will find that he must do both. (Goffman, 1971: 37)

In addition, there is behind the 'front' also the 'interior' management of personal feelings – self-doubt, anxiety or, conversely, pleasures and delights that may be associated with the research going well. While a (research) task may be unfamiliar, there will be pre-existing 'fronts' available to help perform it. Therefore, when 'a task is given a new front we seldom find that the front it is given is itself new' (Goffman, 1971: 37–8). The practice of 'interviewing', for example, may well be new to the researcher. However, he or she (and the 'subjects') will have seen interviews performed (e.g. in the media) or will have been interviewed before (e.g. for the research post or postgraduate course itself, or even previously 'interviewed' by a market researcher or polling organisation by telephone, at the door or on the street). As part of learning 'fronts', the researcher, whether haphazardly, occasionally or systematically, 'self-monitors' his or her research competence and 'presentation', or the extent to which the job is done well and what can be learned for the future. This review of active research involvement is an intrinsic part of research itself rather than a sidelight, and it should be extended 'reflexively'.

As Mills advocates, we should 'learn to use' our biographical experience in our intellectual work. It is an essential ingredient as we continue to 'examine and interpret it' (Mills, 1970: 216). Again, the self-monitoring of the 'performance' and the feelings of the researcher are very different in data collection, according to whether qualitative or quantitative methods are being applied, but is very relevant to both. As Elliott argues:

... the theoretical perspective and intellectual autobiography of the researcher is likely to be just as relevant whether qualitative or quantitative analysis is undertaken. Although the intuitive and interpretive aspects of qualitative analysis are already widely acknowledged ... there needs to be greater recognition that quantitative analysis is by no means a completely routinized and codified process, but rather is also shaped by the decisions made by individual researchers. (Elliott, 2005: 161)

The cultural position of the researcher

In carrying out my research in South Wales, I became increasingly aware of a number of issues surrounding how I was 'constructing' the 'field' and my 'presentational front(s)', including conceptions of participants and setting. Drawing on recent writings on anthropological ethnography and the use of autobiography within sociology, I began to see a number of such issues in my work, including the re-examination of my cultural background and research position in relation to those studied, the challenge to simple distinctions between fieldwork and biography, and the construction and presentation of the 'field' as part of my own 'ethnographic life' (Rose, 1990). As Okely describes:

A fundamental aspect of anthropology concerns the relationships between cultures or groups. The autobiography of the fieldworker anthropologist is neither in a cultural vacuum, nor confined to the anthropologist's own culture, but is instead placed in a cross-cultural encounter. Fieldwork practice is always concerned with relationships. ... The auto-biographical experience of fieldwork requires the deconstruction of those relationships with the rigour demanded elsewhere in the discipline. (Okely, 1992: 2)

It appeared that the more I researched – observed, interviewed, and collected a very diverse range of primary and secondary materials – the more I was cognisant of my own personality and self-presentation. Involved here was my cultural position (as academic, male) and the degree to which I 'shared' common assumptions and outlooks with those in my community study.

Sociological imagination and research practice

Sociological research should be based on an 'openness' and 'awareness' in outlook, as far as possible, in its practice. As C.W. Mills famously described, the 'sociological imagination', as an orientation to research, connects the personal life of the sociologist with the socio-historical context. In my view, Mills's notion can serve as a general guiding formulation for research practice and experience:

Do not allow public issues as they are officially formulated, or troubles as they are privately felt, to determine the problems that you take up for study. ... Know that the problems of social science, when adequately formulated, must include both troubles and issues, both biography and history, and the range of their intricate relations. Within that range the life of the individual and the making of societies occur; and within that range the sociological imagination has its chance to make a difference in the quality of human life in our time. (Mills, 1970: 248)

It is this reflection on the diverse connections between the personal and the social context, biography and history, and the private and the public that makes Mills's conception of the 'imagination' in sociological practice so stimulating on how we 'imagine' ourselves and our activities. We construct 'images' of the situations in which we act. For example, in carrying out research, the investigator begins to learn, according to Becker, a number of the 'tricks of the trade', just as others (e.g. chefs, butlers, managers and doctors) in their occupations find ways of doing things that are effective in meeting problems or perhaps doing the more laborious parts of the job. One such trick involves 'imagery'. He argues that 'our imagery' has an important bearing on the direction of our research – 'the ideas we start with, the questions we ask to check them out, the answers we find plausible'. We do this without a great deal of thought. It merely seems part of our everyday lives and experience. We do not consider such information, which forms our daily existence, in the same way as we would the 'scientific' material in our academic work and publications (Becker, 1998: 12–13). But, often the 'certainties' of our 'ordinary lives' enter into the 'uncertainties' of the field.

Becker's interesting conclusion reflects back from our research and academic pursuits to our broader daily lives:

Since our lay imagery influences our work so much, we should take care that it is accurate. But how can you do that? Imagery enters our heads as the residue of our everyday experience; so, to get better imagery in there, we have to do something about the character of our ordinary lives. (Becker, 1998: 15)

Early days in research

When contemplating a study, the researcher faces a number of questions:

... as soon as researchers begin to examine the research process, they are confronted with many questions: to whom are researchers accountable? To whom are researchers responsible? How do researchers minimise deception? Do researchers inform all informants equally? Do researchers collaborate with informants? Such questions do not have any definite answers. However, a consideration of these problems can help researchers to make informed decisions on the basis of their analysis of the social, ethical and political context of field research. (Burgess, 1982: 237)

The researcher engaged in fieldwork – interviewing, acting as a participant observer, conducting a survey in an organisation or community – enters a new situation that may have some similarities with other new situations experienced previously in other parts of life. But, even if an experienced researcher, the situation will have some 'newness' by having its own social and environmental characteristics. During the research the investigator, whether a novice or one with more experience, will have to develop a number of subtle presentational skills alongside the 'research skills' that textbooks routinely describe. While research can be portrayed as a process of 'data collection', it also exhibits a series of entrances and exits in the contacts with the researched and others, which will have to be timed and approached in the correct manner, according to situation. Research involves forms of 'presentation' by the individual researcher, not merely the application of 'technical recipes' gained from a course or a textbook. It includes attachments, purposes, uncertainties and concerns which bear upon 'self-presentation'. The 'who, what, when, where and how' questions of research raise personal challenges and associated feelings. Additionally, the question 'Why?' in choosing a particular research procedure or topic can go rather deeper, behind the 'presentational front', than is often admitted: even the experienced researcher may often ask 'Why am I doing this research at all?' (see Wilkins, 1993).

Entering research contexts

Entering any research setting, and conducting interviews, distributing questionnaires, participant observation, and so on, entails a degree of anxiety, even trepidation regarding acceptance by others, the possible difficulties to be encountered and whether the research will be completed successfully. Certain settings may create extra concerns, for instance, in the need for more attention to researcher safety, ethical issues related to the use of 'covert' versus 'overt' approaches, or in researching 'divided' or 'captive' communities (see Brewer, 2000; Fielding, 2004). For instance, Davies comments on research in prison settings:

> The period between the preparation and the actual doing of the interviews can be a time of anticipation, which may include moments not only of concern about what lies ahead, but also of fear. Although fieldwork is often a part of the research process to look forward to, doing interviews with known criminals who have apparently done something serious enough to warrant their loss of liberty can still be a daunting prospect. (Davies, 2000: 86)

A number of prisoners in a study may well have committed very serious offences and researchers should be continuously aware of their safety: 'Certainly some inmates are extremely dangerous and continue to commit sometimes serious crime while they are in prison. ... Researchers should be safety conscious at all times' (Martin, 2000: 224). But, as Martin argues, 'assaults on people who work in prisons (with the exception of uniformed officers) are extremely rare – and it is very unusual for researchers to feel unsafe or threatened in any way'. She adds that there is also often 'a style of grim humour which is part of prison life' and working in prisons 'is by no means a dispiriting experience' (Martin, 2000: 224).

Finally, it is quite possible, apart from scrutinising the qualifications of the researcher, that an institution or a group will 'check out' the 'presentational front' or the existing 'reputation' of the researcher in various ways:

This may create complex problems for the researcher in 'passing over' as a legitimate person. There is the likelihood that he or she will be tested and face unofficial rites of passage. As a researcher, it is not uncommon to hear stories from the researched about the character and outcomes of previous research. One example involves comments from senior police officers with regard to a researcher studying victims' and offenders' treatment by the police who is now commonly known in this particular police force as the 'study and snitch' researcher since she seemed to them friendly during the research and then produced what they thought was a damning written report. Whatever the rights and wrongs of this case, it is a useful illustration of the type of informal barriers to access which may be erected by institutions following earlier research experiences. (Hughes, 2000: 241–2)

Entering research

The 'entrance' to the research context can take place in various ways. Contact with participants may be through an introductory letter, a group meeting, a personal introduction, a door-to-door response, an advertisement, and so on. Whyte's *Street Corner Society* (1955) is regarded as a classic community study in sociology. In this book, Whyte outlines in detail his 'entrance' to the 'field' via his famous 'key informant' 'Doc'. The closeness of this researcher–subject relationship was subjected to a later assessment by Whyte, who commented:

The man I called 'Doc' in *Street Corner Society* (1943) was far more to me than an informant in the usual sense of the term. Beginning as my chief guide into the intricacies of Cornerville, he came to be also a

(Continued)

collaborator in the research. We spent many hours discussing what he and I were observing. Piece by piece, he read through the first draft of the book and gave me his detailed criticisms. (Whyte, 1970: 38)

Doc became Whyte's guide to the community and to his group of friends. The relationship became more than that between an observer of communal life and a 'passive informant' (Roberts, 2002: 156). What the study demonstrates, not only for such communal or group studies but also for other research, is that the description of research relations is open for others to assess, describe, interpret, admire or condemn. Whyte later vigorously defended his field methodology and relations with those reported in the study, and his portrait of the community, against subsequent criticisms (Whyte, 1992).

Reasons to research

A wide variety of reasons can be given for starting a particular piece of research or for entering a research career. Usually there is a mix of immediate pragmatic reasons, such as a need for employment or an interest in the area or the work of a research team, and longer-term considerations, probably in relation to gaining skills, qualifications and career aspirations. It may just be because we have some broad reason, such as finding out about the lives of others or making a contribution to social betterment – a general humanistic impulse. But again, to understand social situations more fully requires some sensitivity in approach to the lives of others:

> A person may set out with the best intentions but lack any real awareness of the actual impact of their behaviour on another person. This may result in hurt feelings all-round, as when the over-protective behaviour of a parent has the inadvertent effect of humiliating their son or daughter, or where a person arranges a surprise party for a friend but only succeeds in embarrassing them because they don't like surprises. In short, even if the best interests of all the participants are borne in mind during such emotional exchanges, there is no guarantee that shared satisfaction will result. Such a state of affairs may be achieved only with the utmost delicacy, expertise and flair. That this is actually accomplished on a fairly regular, everyday basis (even if only 'approximately') is a great testament to the skills of ingenuity of most people. (Layder, 2004: 12)

Reasons to research

Numerous reasons can underlie why someone wishes to undertake research or a postgraduate degree thesis (at MA/MSc or doctoral level) (see Leonard, 2001: 50–2 and Potter, 2002b: 14–17). Reasons for all kinds of research can involve the following:

- 'Bugged by an issue' – the researcher may be fascinated by a social issue or topic.
- New developments – the researcher may want to develop a new view or bring existing ideas and theory in one field to a different area.
- Research is a satisfying activity – the researcher may just want to engage in 'research' as an intellectual and practical pursuit.
- Contribution to community and society – the researcher may wish to make a useful contribution to knowledge on a pressing social problem or to make clear the effects of governmental or other decisions on particular groups, or help such groups find a 'voice'.
- Research career – the research post or degree may be a step on the research or academic career ladder. It may also be important for advancement in an existing career (e.g. in health or welfare administration).
- Research qualification – the researcher may seek to gain a qualification as a personal challenge and for a sense of achievement. This may follow earlier setbacks in his or her personal life or educational progress.
- Socially useful skills and knowledge – the researcher may wish to pass on and use the research skills and knowledge gained for the benefit of others within a group or community (e.g. for communal projects).

Asking the question 'Why carry out research?' – in general, or on a particular area, or according to a certain kind of approach – may aid an understanding of our orientation and actions during a study. As far as they are able, postgraduates and other researchers need to be 'honest' with themselves on the degree of self-commitment that is being given, and able to appraise the demands and support of others, such as co-workers and funders (see Blaxter et al., 2001: 9–11). Such evaluations help the researcher assess his or her reasons – and the doubts about the personal and other benefits of study.

The PhD experience

Assessing the reasons for carrying out research is only part of the preparation for future study. Before applying for a research post or a postgraduate place it is wise to do some 'research' on the department and/or institution, and the research team or supervisor. The researcher will need to assess exactly what he or she will be required to do in the research, and what support will be received. Information on the past record of research by the group or the interests of the postgraduate supervisor/supervisory team is also important. If the researcher does not know the institution or the city, then again some research is very advisable to get a 'feel' of both and whether he or she is likely to be at 'home' there.

PhD experience: preparation and adaptation

The keys to the initial stage of doing a PhD (or applying for a research post) are detailed 'preparation' before starting and a successful 'adaptation' to the new way of life when it begins.

Preparation

It is essential to 'look ahead' to your 'new life'. Begin to 'think yourself' into the new situation and make some prior arrangements.

- Reconnoitre the institution and city, and find out about the department and supervisory team.
- Be 'realistic' about what to expect and what adjustments – in living and working – will have to be made.
- If you are unsure whether to take a post or postgraduate place, take further advice and try to gain further information.
- Remember it is not just a work commitment being made but possibly changes in where you are living and in other parts of your life.
- Question, for instance at the interview, whether there will be sufficient support for you materially and in terms of mentoring. Talk, if possible, to other postgraduates.

Adaptation

You will have to make some adaptations to the new environment and new relationships will have to be forged, e.g., with the supervisory team.

- Make friends – join clubs and/or teams in the university.
- Meet other postgraduates to share common interests.

(Continued)

(Continued)

- Keep to a 'normal routine' if possible – treat it as a '9 to 5' job and relax in the evenings.
- Make sure you know the rules and regulations governing your PhD and its supervision.
- Seek advice – on workload, progress, on work drafted, conferences to attend, contacts to make, presentations to give and publications to write.
- There are a number of very useful guides to postgraduate research – read them and adapt them to your situation and feelings (e.g. see Cryer, 2000; Leonard, 2001; Potter, 2002a).
- Remember, while postgraduate research is hard work, and there is 'much perspiration and some inspiration', it is also a very exciting opportunity to explore new ideas and to follow a specific topic in greater depth.

Many of the above comments also fit the situation of the new researcher who is part of a research team.

Engagement in PhD research involves a supervisory team who guides and advises the student on the research process, submission and viva, according to information and regulations set out by the university. The team usually works well and one member will be the 'director of studies' or 'main supervisor'. He or she should make sure that advice is both helpful and consistent so that conflicting messages are not given about the content, standard and organisation of work, and to ensure that regulations are met. However, it may be that a member of the team may seem 'awkward', favouring a particular approach to an issue, or does not seem to respond well to requests for help or to fulfil other duties as a supervisor. If so, then these difficulties need to be addressed early on by discussion with the main supervisor and the team. The PhD student and supervisor should always keep a record of meetings, including work to do and decisions made. If supervision is thought to be insufficient, the researcher should first consider whether he or she expected too much from the team and discuss the problem. After all, it is the researcher's own work which will be judged. Leonard points out that while new researchers may assume that supervisors will direct them to do things, as the research develops they should become more independent and there should be more equal dialogue (Leonard, 2001: 87). The researcher should become more knowledgeable about a specialist area than those supervising or leading a team. There is also a 'subjective side' to research supervision; the researcher must be aware that supervisors are 'human beings' who may have their own workload pressures, and may be relatively inexperienced (Cryer, 2000: 18–19).

A researcher for a postgraduate degree (or other research) will undergo some changes in personal circumstances and routine, and probably in self-definition.

As Cryer emphasises, the postgraduate researcher, in considering undertaking research, should recognise the 'need for adjustment'. She says a 'long research programme has to be a way of life, not just a job, because it cannot simply be locked away into office hours inside the institution or other place of work' (Cryer, 2000: 27). Questions relating to living away from home and parents or partner (and children or dependants), to living with other students, and to health or finance can arise. The focus of the postgraduate or other researcher on the research team can leave less time for home life, and for engagement in routine tasks of caring, myriad household tasks and emotional obligations. In postgraduate research, Leonard says, there are 'general issues of loss of status, lack of money, the need to build a new support system, and the physical effects of changed patterns of diet and exercise, recreation and socialization' (Leonard, 2001: 169; see also Foskett and Foskett, 2006). Changes may be very substantial due to separation from the researcher's cultural background. For instance, foreign students may feel isolated and longing to be back home in a familiar pattern of life. Thus, it is important that commitments are thought through as far as possible in advance and reviewed as the research progresses so that the effects on personal relationships are minimised.

Postgraduate dissertations

Les Back (2002) 'Dancing and wrestling with scholarship: things to do and things to avoid in a PhD career', *Sociological Research Online,* **7 (4)**.

Les Back makes a vivid point concerning the experience of writing a PhD – when it is going well it is like a good dancing partner, but when it's going badly it is like being tossed about as if in some gruelling intellectual wrestling bout.

Back gives useful advice to the PhD student. He points to the PhD as being the start of a certain kind of journey, which sometimes feels 'overwhelming' and 'daunting', with its own beginning and arrival points. Back recommends that the postgraduate student reads a few existing theses in the library. This will show what is expected and that others have managed to complete! He says there is no 'formula' – that is simply filling in the pages according to a pre-set schema. Rather, completing a PhD is a creative process. He recommends a number of aphorisms, drawn from his own experiences as a supervisor and student, to guide the PhD student, although he adds that not all supervisors might agree:

Trust your own interest.
Keep a ledger of your thinking.
Read promiscuously with an open mind.
Don't become addicted to the library.

(Continued)

(Continued)

> Don't be afraid to get close to the thing you're trying to understand.
> Don't become a fieldwork junkie.
> Embrace the challenge of becoming a writer.
> Don't carry the burden of originality.
> Don't try to judge your own work.
> Have faith in the value of what you are doing. (Back, 2002: 3)

Back is right to be cautious about simply following 'rules' or strict schemes. Of course, the formal regulations for PhD submission have to be adhered to, but the actual process of research study is a complex and individual experience.

The challenge of completing a dissertation

Deciding to do a dissertation (or a research report) is not simply 'signing up' for much hard work. It is a commitment that can raise a personal questioning. As Rudestam and Newton argue, 'the challenge of completing an acceptable dissertation may also invoke deeply felt beliefs about incompetence and the inability to master this task'. They say that in their experience 'the dissertation process more often than not stirs up a student's most basic behavioral patterns and emotional vulnerabilities' (Rudestam and Newton, 1992: 134). They outline a range of issues that they have found in their students' work. These can take the form of complex beliefs:

- Work for a PhD will be seen as disloyalty towards family members who did not achieve the same in education.
- The PhD's completion may bring challenges that are frightening and not possible to do.
- Achieving a new status will be a threat to personal relationships.
- Doing a PhD may after all appear to be beyond one's capabilities or really one will turn out to be an impostor or fraud, only seeming to take part.
- The PhD can demand compromises to keenly held ideals to achieve (Rudestram and Newton, 1992: 134–5).

However, Rudestam and Newton report that despite the impediments that might arise: 'We have also been gratified to discover that students can generally identify and access significant coping skills that they may never have realized they possessed' (Rudestam and Newton, 1992: 135).

Research 'hold-ups'

The conduct of research, whether for a dissertation or some other project, brings inevitable frustrations and setbacks, but the presence of a problem or difficulty should not dissuade the researcher from continuing. Often what appears as a 'crisis' today and may lead to a sense of 'panic' is quite readily dealt with and soon passes. Some difficulties occur in any role and do not usually have lasting consequences for feelings of self-confidence and competence. They should be dealt with as calmly and 'logically' as possible and appropriate help and advice sought rather than letting things drift in case of seeming to 'lose face' by admitting problems.

Research 'hold-ups'

Research for a PhD degree or another type of project can extend over a long period. Almost inevitably, there are times when the study does not seem to be going very well and the researcher feels discouraged. There are a number of common research 'hold-ups' and 'hang-ups' that can affect researcher morale:

- Not enough previous preparation
- Loss of energy
- Intrusion of negative feelings – boredom, inadequacy
- Hitches in the research methodology
- Difficulties in relationships with colleagues
- Change of colleagues, creating disruption
- There are too many demands
- Tasks never seem to be properly completed
- Too little time to meet deadlines
- The research seems to lack direction and focus
- Nothing 'new' seems to be emerging
- Overwhelmed by data collected
- Uncertainties regarding the research purpose
- Distractions from outside relationships
- What to do after the research?
- Working on the next research grant proposal
- Already having to start other research (see Cryer, 2000: 212–24)

It may be that the difficulties seem numerous and 'the road long'. Again, research goes through various phases in which some tasks rather than others predominate. Thus, present difficulties, if dealt with, will end. More seriously, it may be felt that the research is 'going nowhere', that the original direction has been lost. It may be that you are trying to do too many things at once, working too hard or trying to rush certain activities – perhaps trying to reach a further stage in the research before completing the necessary intervening steps. Again, a sense of perspective is needed, even a break from the research to refresh mentally and physically. Discussing work difficulties with others, such as colleagues engaged in the same programme, or the supervisory team for the postgraduate degree, is crucial. In this way, the work can be re-planned if necessary, 'drive' can hopefully be restored, and a sense of direction regained.

Key points to remember on researcher experience: entering the research

Research activity can involve important shifts in the organisation of life's activities, routines and commitments:

- Research is 'presentational' as well as 'methodological', 'experiential' as well as 'technical'.
- Research brings new challenges and circumstances – prior preparation and later adaptation in routines and personal life will be necessary.
- There are several reasons for conducting research, ranging from an intense interest in an area to seeking a qualification, or gaining valuable skills or knowledge that can be passed on to others.
- Research brings 'hold-ups' and 'hang-ups'. Some difficulties should be expected. They are often temporary and usually can be readily overcome.

Summary

Entering research is not simply a technical matter of preparing the right methodological techniques. It is also a 'personal' experience. Excitement and apprehension may be mixed together as the researcher considers his or her competence, the stimulation of finding out about a topic and making a contribution to the discipline. The conduct of research can also alter private relationships and how the researcher understands the social world. The reasons for becoming a researcher can be varied and the motivations for carrying out a particular project or a dissertation may change during the study. While it is difficult to lay down a set way of dealing with research experiences, it can be said that some personal preparation by the researcher is necessary prior to research. Also, the researcher's presentation of self is deeply implicated in entering research and in subsequent situations. Getting research commitments into perspective, by seeking advice and a wide range of support, and engaging in social activities, is essential to enable the researcher to enjoy the investigative experience more, and produce a successful report.

Further reading

A general introduction to research conduct is L. Blaxter et al. (2001) *How to Research* (2nd edn, Buckingham: Open University Press). For more specific advice on coping with or surviving a PhD (or other student project) a range of books are now available: J. Bell (1999) *Doing Your Research Project* (3rd edn, Buckingham: Open University Press); D. Burton (ed.) (2000) *Research Training for Social Scientists: A Handbook for Postgraduate Researchers* (London: Sage); P. Cryer (2000) *The Research Student's Guide to Success* (Buckingham: Open University Press); R. Murray (2003) *How To Survive Your Viva* (Maidenhead: Open University Press); Z. O'Leary (2004) *The Essential Guide to Doing Research* (London: Sage); S. Potter (ed.) (2002) *Doing Postgraduate Research* (London: Sage); C.M. Roberts (2004) *The Dissertation Journey* (London: Corwin Press); K.E. Rudestam and R.R. Newton (1992) *Surviving Your Dissertation* (London: Corwin Press; 2nd edn, 2000); and G. Rugg and M. Petre (2004) *The Unwritten Rules of PhD Research* (Maidenhead: Open University Press). A recent text that covers elements of an autobiographical approach is C. Seale et al. (eds) (2004) *Qualitative Research Practice* (London: Sage). See also, on the self in research, N. Hallowell et al. (eds) (2005) *Reflections on Research* (Maidenhead: Open University Press) and J. Okely and H. Callaway (eds) (1992) *Anthropology and Autobiography* (London: Routledge).

5

INTERPRETATION IN RESEARCH

Chapter overview

The researcher as interpreter/theorist
The research diary
Data, and yet more data
Organising interpretations and new ideas
Key points to remember on researcher experience: interpretation in research
Summary
Further reading

... the auto/biographical 'I' signals the active inquiring presence of sociologists in constructing, rather than discovering, knowledge. (Stanley, 1993: 41)

So you've got your data, maybe a stack of completed questionnaires, a pile of interview transcripts, a mound of relevant documents, as well as your own research journal – some of which is even legible! The question now is what are you going to do with it? ... There is NO substitute for the insight, acumen, and common sense – or the 'mother-wit' you will need to manage the process. ... In short, researchers need to keep a keen sense of their overall project and think their way through analysis. (O'Leary, 2004: 184)

The researcher as interpreter/theorist

A fuller understanding of the process of interpretation begins with the recognition of the place of the researcher as interpreter/theorist. Denzin, in relation to qualitative research, says that the researcher 'is not an objective, politically neutral observer who stands outside and above the study of the social world'. In this view, the researcher's interpretative practice can be seen as 'historically and locally situated within the very processes being studied' (Denzin, 2001: 3). For Denzin, arguing that all research interpretation depends on a 'positioning' of the researcher challenges the traditional model of interpretative work portrayed in 'scientific' endeavour:

> In the social sciences today there is no longer a God's-eye view that guarantees absolute methodological certainty. All inquiry reflects the standpoint of the inquirer. All observation is theory-laden. There is no possibility of theory – or value-free knowledge. The days of naïve realism and naïve positivism are over. In their place stand critical and historical realism as well as various versions of relativism. The criteria for evaluating research are now relative. This is the nonfoundational position. (Denzin, 2001: 3)

The researcher, following Denzin, should think of him or herself as a 'interpreter/theorist', 'constructing' an account from the 'materials', notes taken, experiences and reflections on research practice. The investigator does not merely 'collect' information but is intimately part of the combined process of forming, shaping and interpreting it. Research interpretation by whatever means (outlet and form) should be interesting, stimulating and possibly, in some cases, 'disturbing' in its effect. While the researcher is very much part of the 'gathering' and 'organising' of research materials, the interpretative outcomes are not always what the researcher and audience may expect, being sometimes contrary to firm assumptions and expectations. Finally, in constructing interpretations, researchers should explore new and multiple means of presenting the research (audio, visual, on the Web, or other means) while 'being alive' to the advantages of disadvantages of such portrayals and the range and manner of 'voices' (researcher and researched) that are given.

The research diary

The file or journal is an essential aid to reflection on past and present (and possible future) experience. The research diary or log is commonly associated with more qualitative types of research. It is used for note-taking on events in the 'field', but also as a record of the research process – ideas, comments, decisions, feelings, jobs done and to do. However, such a record is not limited to qualitative methodology; it can also be an important part of quantitative research (e.g. surveys), documentary and unobtrusive research, although (so far) less likely to be commented upon in such reportage. For Mills, the research file organises and guides the 'intellectual craftsman' [sic] in systematic reflection (Mills, 1970: 216):

> … there is joined personal experience and professional activities, studies under way and studies planned. In this file, you, as an intellectual craftsman, will try to get together what you are doing intellectually and what you are experiencing as a person. Here you will not be afraid to use your experience and relate it directly to various work in progress. (Mills, 1970: 216)

The personal diary or log

A detailed personal log is an important record of researcher experience which, for Mills, is an essential part of being an 'intellectual craftsman'. It provides the following:

- It records strong feelings about events rather than losing them from your mind.
- By 'developing self-reflective habits, you learn how to keep your inner world awake'.
- It allows the formulation and 'drawing out' of feelings.
- It enables some evaluation of feelings – how 'foolish' the ideas are or how 'they might be articulated into productive shape'.
- 'The file also helps you build up the habit of writing. You cannot "keep your hand in" if you do not write something at least every week'.
- 'In developing the file, you can experiment as a writer' and so 'develop your powers of expression'.
- To 'maintain a file is to engage in the controlled experience' (Mills, 1970: 217).

Even so, note-taking may not always be systematic and notes may not always be compiled under the best of circumstances. As Rose reveals: 'I transcribed field notes at night sometimes too drunk to focus well, or worked on them the next morning, more sober and less close to what had gone on the day before' (Rose, 1990: 13).

Note-taking on the conduct of the research is therefore a vital writing activity. Burgess describes it as 'a personal activity that depends upon the research context, the objectives of the research and relationships with informants' (Burgess, 1982: 191).

A file, log or diary on research activities can be extended as part of all research – not only fieldwork (itself a collection of methods) but also more quantitatively based research, such as survey questionnaires and more formal interviews. These latter forms of research also take place over time and involve choices, decisions, reflections, insights and observations within the research process.

Kleinman and Copp (1991) argue that there are dangers in 'cutting corners' on what has to be written down, say about an interview and its setting, even if noting 'everything' in a diary seems to be an endless recording of trivia. Later, certain details noted may begin to take on a 'sociological importance', so decisions regarding what is deemed interesting or not can have a bearing on later interpretative-theoretical work. Again, our mood can have a direct effect on how we conduct research at a given moment (Kleinman and Copp, 1991: 23).

Types of fieldnotes

Burgess usefully outlines a variety of possible fieldnotes.

Substantive fieldnotes. These give the description of the context of the research in which the data was collected. Attention is to the 'main observations, conversations and interviews which the researcher makes'. Included here are the 'lists of names, dates, places and events' and 'in the case of documentary work, details on the content of documents'.

Methodological fieldnotes. For Burgess it is 'important to keep records on personal impressions of situations and personal involvement'. The researcher notes the 'details concerning field roles, the selection of informants, relationships with informants and some self-analysis that gives an account of emotional relationships at various points throughout the research process'.

Analytic fieldnotes. Fieldwork notes should include any 'preliminary analysis' as 'brief indicators to the researcher about topics that can be developed, themes that can be explored and brief details of analysis ... the researcher has to code and classify field notes as the research proceeds' (Burgess, 1982: 192–3).

There is something of a continuum or contrast in regard to types of fieldnotes and the degree of the 'inner thoughts' or the revelations they give on research experience (see Kleinman and Copp, 1993: 26). On the one hand, they may give the various feelings the researcher has towards the research process, the 'subjects', others in the research team, the research supervisor and his or her own feelings of 'self'. Such thoughts may form a series of notes or a daily diary, much of which is not intended for publication. On the other hand, the more detail contained in research notes on the central issues of theorisation and methodology, the more they can be expected to inform the finished report, article, conference paper or book. Traditionally, the interpretation process tends to 'edit out' the 'subjective side' for the ostensible reasons of ethics, sense of privacy, or the conventional and expected principles of research reporting. The 'inside' story of research is usually erased.

Research diaries can be used by the researcher for self-expression, self-exploration and 'self-analysis'. At a later date, such diaries, which were meant to be 'private' observations, can be very revealing of the researcher's feelings towards him or herself, and those researched (e.g. the famous case of Malinowski's diary). Also, letters may be written and consulted later, for instance, in the case of Margaret Mead and her reflections on her field activities (Burgess, 1982: 192). Today the noting of field activities and reflections can be aided by the (digital) tape recorder, the video camera, mobile phone (using video, image and text), photographs and even direct to a hand-held computer. Internet weblogs, with appropriate ethical safeguards, can draw on these means to give sound, images and text recording of the research setting, to which others can respond. Burgess concludes that the field researcher may write notes or diaries (containing plans, diagrams and other content) alongside interview transcripts, tape and video recordings and photographs. He adds that whatever is collected, 'it is essential for them to be maintained systematically, as the record of field experiences are the detail out of which theoretical, methodological and substantive discussions are constructed in the final research report' (Burgess, 1982: 193).

Finally, Mills, in pointing to 'accomplished thinkers' who 'closely observe their development' and 'treasure their smallest experience', stresses the imperative to record research activity. Such note-writing is an important source of original intellectual work:

To be able to trust yet to be sceptical of your own experience, I have come to believe, is one mark of the mature workman [sic]. This ambiguous confidence is indispensable to originality in any intellectual pursuit, and the file is one way by which you can develop and justify such confidence. (Mills, 1970: 217)

Data, and yet more data

As the research process develops, the task of interpretation for the final report, the dissertation, book or presentation comes more into view. The uncertainties of collecting enough research material are translated into a concern that there is just too much to analyse and interpret and eventually transform into the finished 'product'. Questions arise in the researcher's mind regarding competence in 'honing' the material into a framework, exacerbated by the feeling perhaps that while there has been success in gathering a mass of collected material, it does not appear to have any 'sense'. The routine collection of more and more material and initial organising seems to be a great deal easier than finding the means to interpret it.

There is something very self-satisfying in viewing recorded materials, notes and other materials filling draws or computer files – the piles of survey questionnaires safely coded, the interview texts organised and stored, and other documents given a place ready for further work. There is a sense of achievement from jobs completed. When amassing materials, there is the temptation to collect more material and record more observations as such work gives a sense of routine, continuity and an immersion in the task. We may become overly intent on recording all or certain aspects of the research, fearful that something may be missed which will be necessary when the main interpretative writing takes place. Collection and filing may also give us a sense of importance and responsibility, such as 'capturing' a context, a set of social relations or a social problem, or even making us a 'recorder' of history. However, again, we should be wary of such tendencies since getting more and more 'data' can put off the assessment of what has been obtained.

Organising interpretations and new ideas

Usually, the process of 'interpretation' is considered to be a particular phase of research, following the organisation of findings. However, 'interpretation' should also be seen as an activity, while focused on a particular phase, that takes place throughout the research process, as the researcher 'interprets' a setting, has expectations of respondents and findings, and begins writing up and reportage. As Okely, an anthropologist, observes:

> ... the interpretation of anthropological material is, like fieldwork, a continuing and creative experience. The research has combined action and contemplation. Scrutiny of the notes offers both empirical certainty and intuitive reminders. Insights emerge also from the subconscious and from bodily memories, never penned on paper. There are serendipitous connections to be made, if the writer is open to them. Writing and analysis comprise a movement between the tangible and intangible, between the cerebral and sensual, between the visible and invisible. Interpretation moves from evidence to ideas and theory, then back again. There can be no set formulae, only broad guidelines, sensitive to specific cases. The researcher is freed from a division of labour which splits fieldwork from analysis. The author is not alienated from the experience of participant observation, but draws upon it both precisely and amorphously for the resolution of the completed text. (Okely, 1994: 32)

In short, ideas (thoughts, notions, concepts) on a substantive research topic can occur prior, during and after the collection of research material. Insights into the research materials can come about from connections made between a wide variety of sources: general personal experiences and change, reading, discussion, reflection and through re-reading old research notes, conference papers and other presentations. Okely describes how thoughts emerged about her research when out walking or during the night; it seemed that ideas and theories had 'fermented in the subconscious' and came out during moments often quite separate from working at the study desk (Okely, 1994: 31–2).

The practice of interpretation and 'analysis of data', therefore, is not simply the application of a set of techniques or routines but it requires thought and creativity. As O'Leary argues:

Good research is a thinking person's game. It is a creative and strategic process that involves constantly assessing, reassessing, and making decisions about the best possible means for obtaining trustworthy information, carrying out appropriate analysis, and drawing credible conclusions. (O'Leary, 2004: 1)

Interpretation and imagination

The process of interpretation is not a simple 'mechanical' exercise but involves 'imagination' – connections, choices, insights. 'Fact-gathering' – the use of statistical methods and procedures, the construction and administration of questionnaires, the forming of interview schedules and interviewing, the compilation of documents (texts and images) – also requires 'thought'. But, the resulting materials do not simply 'speak for themselves', they need some further imaginative, interpretative work. They are 'made sense of' by arranging and sorting – the procedures adopted, and the insights and theoretical associations made. The process of interpretation, as in other aspects of the research, can be challenging, but it can also create a great deal of excitement as different interpretations are explored, conceptualisation and theorisation take place, and comparisons are made with previous studies.

Becker (1998) is very informative about the role of the imagination and the 'imagery' used by the social scientist. However, he cautions that as we 'all claim to be social *scientists*, we don't stop with imagination and extrapolation, as a novelist or filmmaker might'. We know 'that our stereotypes are just that, and are as likely to be inaccurate as not'. He adds, quoting Blumer:

[T]he research scholar in the social sciences has another set of pre-established images that he [*sic*] uses. These images are constituted by his theories, by the beliefs current in his own professional circles, and by his ideas of how the empirical world must be set up to allow him to follow his research procedure. No careful observer can honestly deny that this is true. We see it clearly in the shaping of pictures of the empirical world to fit one's theories, in the organizing of such pictures in terms of the concepts and beliefs that enjoy current acceptance among one's set of colleagues, and in the molding of such pictures to fit the demands of scientific protocol. (Becker, 1998: 13)

Imagination and interpretation take place in all research practice. Within qualitative research methodology a wide range of interpretative or analytic models have been employed, and there is a very large body of discussion on their characteristics and merits. These include, for example, analytic induction, grounded theory, and thematic analysis. There are also various computer programs that aid qualitative analysis. Serious and complex debates have taken place concerning the extent to which 'concepts' and 'theories' prefigure or direct the collection of qualitative materials, are uncovered or constructed within material, or 'found' after the material or 'facts' have been gathered. In quantitative research, similarly, there are numerous kinds of (statistical) analyses whose use is anticipated or resorted to after the material is amassed, and extensive guidance on techniques is given in major methodological textbooks. In both qualitative and quantitative research, not only are decisions to be made regarding the models or statistical analyses/tests to be employed, but the meaning and importance of the findings still have to be discerned. Included here is the further linkage with existing research findings and theorisation on the topic or issue. Across the process of interpretation, imagination has to be employed in constructing the meaning of the research, from the shaping or organising of research materials, concept formation or application, through to theorisation.

Interpretation can raise a sense of trepidation: 'Will the research aims be met?' 'How am I going to make sense of what has been found?' 'Will I have found something interesting or important, and produced an explanation that is tenable and coherent?' It can be an arduous task and it may be frustrating 'to find a way through' the material or have alternative understandings and explanations arise. But, 'playing' with different theoretical possibilities or ways of seeing a social issue or context is very stimulating. The act of interpretation can foster a heightened feeling and commitment to what the research set out to do and what is being achieved.

The process of interpretation can be a long-lasting one, including the remembrance of research – the retrospective gaze, perhaps some years later, may not only lead to a re-living of earlier emotions felt during the investigation but may also give a 'new' perspective to the original research. Robert Moore, in a reflective account of his multi-method community research with John Rex (Rex and Moore, 1967), recalls their later feelings:

> When we were finishing *Race, Community and Conflict* ... John Rex and I often remarked how we should each write our Sparkbrook novel. This was not because either of us had lost faith in sociology; it was rather an expression of our need to communicate something of our response to Sparkbrook as a human situation, filled with humour, conflict, hardship and affection. (Moore, 1977: 87)

These comments, although retrospective (and he was aware of the dangers of recasting his experiences), do give some of the variety of emotional experiences that can exist in research and how it can 'live on'. Okely (1994) also shows that our research 'stays with us' as we reflect back and re-interpret it via our own thoughts, discussions with others in and outside work, and later presentations or in teaching. The research undertaken months, if not years, before has become part of our own biographical understanding and 'new meaning' can be 'found' (Okely, 1994: 31–2). Okely gives a more 'realistic' light on the process of interpretation than usually given:

Ideas may emerge from only the most intangible link with recorded notes. They arise in part as a response to other theories and ideas, long after fieldwork. For example, when the first book had been sent to press, and I was no longer employed by the policy-oriented research centre but instead registered for a doctorate and in the very different atmosphere of a university anthropology department, new ways of thinking about my fieldwork and the Gypsies took shape. (Okely, 1994: 31)

Re-interpretation and re-study: the return of the researcher to the field

Autobiographical experiences that help in shaping the practice of research are in themselves very complex and subject to re-interpretation while being in an interplay with the unfolding research. In research we are often within sets of relationships with others and at the same time in a relation with our own past, present and future perceptions or understandings (in our academic research and in our 'outside' lives). Research activity is a period that is very much part of an ongoing life process. As Kenna found, following her fieldwork on a Greek island as a young novice researcher in the 1960s and then returning 20 years later: 'Changes in age, status and stage in the life cycle have altered my own perspectives and affected both fieldwork experience and analysis. Each successive backward look offers a refocusing of its object. Autobiography, like history, is constantly being rewritten' (Kenna, 1992: 161; see also Brewer, 2000: 99–101).

The concerns of the young, female, researcher at the start of her career with a particular academic socialisation and the reactions of members of the community had changed on her 'return to the field', and her earlier work was subject to review and re-evaluation with hindsight. This 'revisiting' should not lead us to give up such autobiographical considerations as too complicated and fraught. Rather, it shows how the ethnographic study can be structured and that the researcher perspective (as developing within the life course) can

(Continued)

be a 'resource'. The personal biographical concerns and life stage of the researcher may provide limits but also insights into the lives of others. The gender and status of the researcher, in Kenna's account, was not merely a 'constraint'. The types of relations of the community members to the 'outsider' provided evidence and insights into the life patterns and concerns of those studied.

Later reflections on the research diary

The later reading of research notes, report or materials, sometimes years later, bring back the experience of the research. Researchers' personal notes, particularly when re-read, may stimulate a re-emergence of earlier feelings. As Bell reminisces:

> I kept a very detailed diary for the first three months of the fieldwork; when I reread it now it still conveys to me the mixture of excitement and boredom we faced. I still recall those months as some of the most interesting of my life. Yet the diary also records a lot of the trivial irritations. (Bell, 1977: 51)

Middleton found the re-reading of her 'field journal' brought 'back in sharp focus all the early uncertainties and worries, and the later grief at having to leave what had become a valued home' (Middleton, 1978: 238).

The re-reading of research notes or diaries can also generate something 'new' as different thoughts, ideas and feelings may emerge as the researcher's subsequent and immediate experiences provide a new context for the 're-reading'.

Key points to remember on researcher experience: interpretation in research

- The researcher is not simply a collector of facts and reporter of findings, but an interpreter/theorist.
- Forms of interpretation can take place throughout research and even after a report is completed.
- While interpretation can be daunting and arduous, it is also exciting, stimulating and rewarding.

Summary

A research diary is an excellent means of 'monitoring' personal feelings, recording conceptual insights, and planning the next research tasks. Interpretation involves the exercise of 'imagination'. The researcher as interpreter/theorist comes to the act of interpretation with a series of expectations and anticipations based on previous personal experiences, research and academic activity. Interpretation is not limited to a particular research phase, but takes place before, during and after the 'gathering' of materials – and even retrospectively, possibly a long time after the research has been completed.

Further reading

T. Benton and I. Craib (2001) *Philosophy of Social Science* (Basingstoke: Palgrave Macmillan) provides a very 'accessible' introduction to the different philosophical perspectives (empiricism and positivism, interpretative perspectives, feminism, hermeneutics and critical reasoning) of the social world. Major textbooks on qualitative and quantitative methods commonly address issues of interpretation, handling data or analysis. A very useful text on the management of data is by Z. O'Leary (2004) *The Essential Guide to Doing Research* (London: Sage), Chapters 1 and 12. A short introduction to the 'steps' involved in interpretation is provided by N.K. Denzin (2001) *Interpretive Interactionism* (2nd edn, London: Sage).

6

WRITING RESEARCH

Writing was the method through which I constituted the world and reconstituted myself. (Richardson, in Denzin, 2001: 155)

The postmodern moment has arrived in the social sciences. Its presence is especially felt in qualitative research circles where calls for new forms of ethnography, polyvocal texts, multigenre narratives, impressionistic tales, cinematic reconstructions, lyrical sociology, and poetic anthropology are prominent. There are, of course, at least as many reasonable justifications for textual experimentation as there are advocates for alterations; but all calls for reform – modest or sweeping – point to a growing lack of confidence among readers across the social sciences with traditional research and reporting styles. (Van Maanen et al., 1990: 5)

Academic writing as a genre

Conventional academic writing can be conceived broadly as a genre:

There are many different genres of writing, including poetry, short-story writing, and formal legal English and business writing. These different styles of writing each have their own characteristics. In much the same way, academic writing is a particular genre, with its own distinctive style, forms of expression and vocabulary. The skills of academic writing can be learned, and anyone who wants to improve their academic writing can acquire such skills. (Oliver, 2004: 13–14)

In general, academic writing should be exact in use of terms and have a good sense of connection: it 'makes clear the linkages between the different aspects of the subject being described or analysed' (Oliver, 2004: 14). These strictures apart, academic writing has reflected a certain tradition and set of assumptions: 'This tradition dictates that academic tomes are generally crafted to appear sober and bookish in their seriousness. They contain pages filled with structured and inconspicuous text that flows from beginning to end without interruption' (Day, 2002: 2.2).

A glance at journals in sociology reveals a general format for articles, including an abstract, key terms, argument and outline of issue(s), previous research and literature, description of the study, implications (e.g. in terms of existing research and theory), and conclusion. Interestingly, writing 'formats' and 'style' even within a single discipline change over time. More recently, this 'academic tradition' has been confronted by new forms of academic writing which overtly and deliberately use a range of genres and insert the 'I' or the 'personal voice' of the investigator into the research account:

… interpretive researchers often feel that it is permissible, and even desirable, to write at least partially in the first person, in order to explain the particular orientation which they bring to the research process. Such reflexive accounts are often seen as being a very desirable element in accounts of interpretive research. Thus, as in all genres of writing, one cannot say that conventions are fixed and rigid. It is probably more accurate to see them as evolving, in parallel with developments in newer approaches to research. (Oliver, 2004: 14)

More broadly, a 'multi-genre' or 'intertextual approach' to writing has been advocated. This disrupts traditional principles, including the set role of the 'objective' researcher, 'as authors engage in dialogue and negotiation with their readers while experimenting with new and unpredictable (and increasingly electronic) textual formats' (Day, 2002: 2.2).

New writing practices and representation

It is becoming more acceptable in research writing to recognise and use various 'writing practices' deriving from a range of other disciplines: to include the first person ('I') and a range of 'genres' (e.g. literary forms of writing within the 'text') and photographs, drawings or other material. Also explored are 'performative' modes of representation, and a conscious inclusion of 'fictive' elements and a movement between fiction and fact. The internet is also giving further possibilities, with video and source links, new forms of discussion, and weblog materials. Sparkes (2002) gives a detailed examination not only of types of 'tale' (scientific, realist and confessional), but also other types of research writing (and performance), including auto/ethnography, poetic representations, ethnodrama and fictional representations. As he argues, choosing an alternative genre does not necessarily provide for a 'better product'. Of course, some researchers question whether drawing, for instance, on literary or performative forms make for 'real research' writing. At the very least, as Sparkes notes, it does raise issues of standards and judgement.

Sparkes (2002) argues, in relation to the study of sport and physical activity, that the increase in new writing practices 'signals a growing awareness in this community that there is no single way, much less one "right" way, to stage a text or to know about a phenomenon'. The modes are 'challenging' and may appear to be 'threatening to more traditionally oriented researchers' (Sparkes, 2002: 225–6):

> Engaging in new writing practices can be risky, but the task is not impossible. Different kinds of tales are being produced, often by young scholars, and they are being published ... [researchers] should take courage from the advances that have been made in this area and not be deterred from experimenting. (Sparkes, 2002: 227)

Sparkes makes a number of 'cautionary points' regarding the adoption of 'new' writing practices:

- Some writers have 'warned that a preoccupation with style and genre runs the risk of aestheticism in which the value of writing about research exhausts itself in the pleasure of the text'.
- Where writing reflects an 'aestheticism' there 'is the risk of elevating style, or panache, over content'.
- Not everyone will be attracted to 'experimental forms of writing' outside the 'standard style'.
- The variety of writing forms ('repertoire of tales') 'gives qualitative researchers both the luxury and the problem of choice'.
- 'If, in many ways, the experience does in part choose the form of representation to make its presence felt' so, qualitative researchers 'may have no option but to tell different tales'. (Sparkes, 2002: 230–3)

Sparkes raises the need for an awareness by researchers of the consequences of choosing the means of representation in terms of type of text or other kind of form: 'Our texts can no longer be taken to be innocent or neutral' (Sparkes, 2002: 233).

Researchers provide a 'structuring' of their research studies through their 'systematic procedures' and writing. Bruyn, referring to participant observation, states:

The character of the world is reflected in the scientific process of knowing, which has form, system, and structure. The structured study thus mirrors itself in its findings. ... Studies in participant observation reveal a variety of research styles with regard to subject matter. Some researchers do not realize that what they discover is shaped by what they themselves are – their temperaments, perspectives, attitudes, and social and personal interests. They have often been unconscious of how these human elements affect their receptivity to the wealth of stimuli capable of reaching them in their research setting. They also have been largely unconscious of the effect upon their own perspectives of current professional styles. Yet these human influences must be understood as a methodological part of social research if the people who are studied are to be understood adequately. Some of the styles which have been evident in past studies are: 1. romantic, 2. realistic, 3. poetic, 4. factual, 5. analytic, 6. satiric, 7. journalistic, and 8. existential. (Bruyn, 1966: 244–5)

Thus, how method and theory are understood and linked is connected to the way the text is written: the text is not a simple reflection of the research activity or the 'reality' that was experienced and researched (Atkinson, 1990: 178). Atkinson, in his analysis of the variety of genres employed in ethnographic studies, says that researchers should not rush out and take up writing in some alternative literary mode. Instead, they should recognise that there are styles of writing, which are 'understood' by a readership, even when more 'factual' information is being delivered (Atkinson, 1990: 180). New forms of writing, in turn, necessitate new attention to the nature of 'reading':

Not only do we need to cultivate a self-conscious construction of ethnographic texts, but also a readiness to *read* texts from a more 'literary-critical' perspective. Sociologists and their students must cultivate the discipline of reading their own and others' arguments for their stylistic and rhetorical properties. (Atkinson, 1990: 180)

Research interpretation can be written up in traditional forms (an article, thesis, book, etc.) which themselves contain various means of expression (description, metaphor, dialogue) and situate the researcher's 'I' in time. It can also be expressed in 'performance' such as the giving of a conference paper. But, research can also be written in less orthodox ways – as performed (and recorded) in poetry, as a play, or in recitation. Here, we can see the blurring of the boundaries of 'fact' and 'fiction', while recognising that 'traditional' reporting of research is itself multi-genre, a mix of various lements ('fact', 'interpretation'), and cannot be a full representation of individuals, social contexts and events.

The various ways of representation lead to questions regarding how to report the research experience, including the process of writing:

> Now, however, more researchers acknowledge the difficulty with allegiance to objectivity. Research methodologists ... have advocated for use of the researcher experience in experiential analysis, heuristic research, and phenomenological nursology, respectively. In addition, anthropologist Ruth Behar ... and sociologist Susan Krieger ... have led efforts to demonstrate how the research experience can be included in research reporting ... [and] argue that the researcher experience is present, no matter how much researchers try to ignore the presence of the researcher within the research report. (Moch, 2000b: 128)

Rose (1990) gives an idea of the kind of 'writing', at least from a qualitative research point of view, that may well become more prevalent. It will include not only the researcher's voice but also a range of genres, writing and media forms – in short, new avenues of 'representation' of the research practice and context: 'I would argue that the future of ethnography – whether in sociology, anthropology, psychology, critical legal studies, planning, or folklore – will be a polyphonic, heteroglossic, multigenre construction' (Rose, 1990: 56). He argues that the 'voice' of the researcher-writer will be present in the representation of research, including 'emotional reactions'. The 'conversations, voices, attitudes, visual genres, gestures, reactions, and concerns of daily life of the people with whom the author participates, observes, and lives will take form as a narrative and discourse in the text – *there will be a story line'* (original italics). Instead of merely 'prose', 'poetics' as well as 'pictures, photos, and drawings will take up a new, more interior relation to the text – not to illustrate it, but to document in their own way what words do in their own way'. Thus, these are 'new possibilities' for authorship and voices: 'the junctures between analytic, fictive, poetic, narrative, and critical genres will be marked clearly in the text but will cohabit the same volume' (Rose, 1990: 57; see also Denzin, 2001). Such developments have been described as part of a 'seventh moment' in (qualitative) research which has brought an openness towards new forms of representation and a 'blurring' of 'interpretive genres' (Denzin and Lincoln, 2000b: 6–7). Denzin and Lincoln (2000b) argue that interpretive writing seeks to share something of the experiences of the research with a reader who can relate it to his or her own experiences. By ensuring versimilitude in research writing, the reader can partake imaginatively in the lives of other individuals (see also Denzin, 2003: Chapter 5).

Again, an issue implicated here is the degree to which reporting research using various styles of writing and forms employ 'fiction' or 'fact'. To what extent is it 'permissible' to mix 'fact' and 'fiction', and thereby, develop 'fictional' characters, events and experiences. Traditional research practice and writing would not accept a trend towards fiction, while those using new practices point to the variety of styles and the 'construction' of the research context and findings that takes place in existing reporting. Here are deep issues regarding 'evaluation', 'judgement', ethics and research purposes (see Hatch and Wisniewski, 1995; Sparkes, 2002: Chapter 9). The researcher has to reflect very carefully on the kind of writing and 'performance' under-taken, what is intended by it and the implications for self, the 'subjects', and audiences. In writing up, the investigator is trying to inform others about the basis of the study and give a 'convincing account' in drawing out conclu-sions. Denzin (2001), in pointing to a broadening of how research can be represented and communicated, draws attention to a 'performative turn' in the social sciences. This opening up of research methodology and dissemi-nation not only produces issues concerning the blurring of fact and fiction (i.e. questions of 'evidence', 'replicability', and so on) but, in addition, more specific problems. Questions relating to how to 'construct, perform, and critically analyze performance texts' (e.g. a theatrical performance based on a research project), and the 'co-participation' between performers and audi-ence (and, perhaps, the researched) come to the fore (Denzin, 2001: 15).

Writing and relations with others

Research writing can be done alone or with others in various ways; it can be carried out with other colleagues who may or may not have had the same close connection with the data gathering or other parts of the project. It may also be written under the guidance of a PhD or other research supervisor, or, unusually, even those studied may have some input, perhaps in the final writ-ing processes (e.g. by giving some feedback on written drafts). Book series edi-tors, proof-readers, journal editors and referees also have a role in what is produced before publication. The kinds of relations between research writers, editors and others usually follow certain well-worn paths. Book and journal publishers have detailed guidelines on format and the kinds of writing to be expected, which may make it difficult, if not impossible, to write in a some-what different manner. However, as Ramazanoğlu argues

As young researchers, we were required to express ourselves in an impersonal style intended to convey the objectivity and validity of our conclusions. ... But conventions of any genre can be disrupted and radical critiques of method generally allow for authors to make their presence felt throughout the research process. (Ramazanoğlu, 2002: 162)

Ramazanoğlu cautions that 'the point of presenting your findings is to be persuasive, and disruption of conventions may or may not serve your purpose' (Ramazanoğlu, 2002: 163).

Day (2002), in her study of how 'computer-mediated communication technologies influence human communication processes in organisational settings', points to some of the difficulties, as a PhD student, in trying to write in a different way:

> In terms of the relationships I had with my supervisors, some facets of these expert/novice dynamics arose especially when I sought to venture away from more traditional ideas regarding what a thesis should be. I tested this need for permission in regard to my desire to include my journal extracts within the thesis and my two academic supervisors responded in significantly different ways. (Day, 2002: 3.1)

She 'negotiated' which extracts should be included and selected ten journal pieces that could be part of the submitted thesis. She also negotiated 'family artworks' related to her research involvement for inclusion (Day, 2002: 4.3). She uses the terms 'Me', 'myself' and 'I' to indicate the variety of stories involved in the formation of narrative and to demonstrate the myriad of personal experiences – hence the use of the term, 'my*self' (Day, 2002: 1.1).

Research writing is, therefore, a complex process. Tedlock outlines some of this intricacy in relation to ethnography and ethnographic representation:

> Ethnography involves an ongoing attempt to place specific encounters, events, and understandings into a fuller, more meaningful context. It is not simply the production of new information or research data, but rather the way in which such information or data are transformed into a written or visual form. ... The ongoing nature of fieldwork connects important personal experiences with an area of knowledge; as a result, it is located between the interiority of autobiography and the exteriority of cultural analysis. (Tedlock, 2000: 455)

She argues that ethnographers have realised that the 'human sciences', instead of attempting to become a natural science, should see themselves as 'multiple sciences': 'The realm of meaning is emergent from the material and organic strata rather than a product of them.' She says that the movement from an 'objectifying methodology' towards a development of an 'intersubjective methodology' involves a 'representational transformation' in research writing (Tedlock, 2000: 471).

In the light of the increasing use of new forms of writing, including the blurring of genres, the researcher is more aware of the issue of 'representation' in writing (and performance). Again, a very important avenue for new forms of writing (and audio-visual presentation) by researchers is the increasing use of the internet, where 'ongoing' research can be reported and comments, advice and interpretations received, and further interaction (between researcher, researched and audience) can take place. Research weblogs, with appropriate procedures for access and participation, will become an important forum for sharing research experience and activities before, during and after research. In fact, the use of weblogs may lead to a blurring between researcher, researched and audience as the timing of research phases become more disrupted and the process more interactive between all involved in the research. Basic issues will remain, particularly, power relations, ethics, accountability and funding. For the researcher, entailed here is not merely an awareness of the new possibilities in representing the research, but the need for new skills in writing and performance. Of course, not every study will (or can) explore a wide range of genres.

Research autobiographies and auto/ethnography

There are a number of books which have reported the research autobiographies of sociological researchers (Merton, 1988; Riley, 1988; see also Hallowell et al., 2005; Seale et al., 2004). These autobiographies report the career influences of other writers, the ideas of others, the movement between institutions, publications, the research communities and what contribution researchers believe they have made to the discipline or sub-discipline. For example, William Foote Whyte summarised his career, his publications and the impact of his work as follows:

Up to this point, I feel that I have had little impact upon the development of general theory in sociology. I have contributed more to methodology in writing about field methods and the role of the participant observer. Perhaps the publication of *Street Corner Society* helped to set off the boom in small group research. I have certainly played a role in shaping the field of industrial sociology or organizational behavior, through my writing and through the students who have worked with me. (Whyte, 1970: 46)

Whyte's article and similar autobiographical statements generally focus on professional and institutional life (e.g. moves in career, research projects undertaken, books published) rather than the intimacies of colleague relations or external influences and life outside academia.

The notion of 'auto/ethnography' has gained prominence in recent years (see Reed-Danahay, 1997). In broad terms, it refers to the very personal account that the researcher gives of the research practice and his or her place within it. Such writing is intended to provide the reader with a deeper knowledge of the researcher's actions, and the research process and relations. In going beyond traditional accounts of research it moves between conventions of differing disciplines while also posing significant questions for assumptions regarding what is 'research'.

Autoethnography is an autobiographical genre of writing and research that displays multiple layers of consciousness, connecting the personal to the cultural. Back and forth autoethnographers gaze, first through an ethnographic wide-angle lens, focusing outward on social and cultural aspects of their personal experience; then, they look inward, exposing a vulnerable self that is moved by and may move through, refract, and resist cultural interpretations. ... As they zoom backward and forward, inward and outward, distinctions between the personal and cultural become blurred, sometimes beyond distinct recognition. (Ellis and Bochner, 2000: 739)

The exact definition of auto/ethnography is difficult due to its development, particularly from social anthropology, into a number of forms and sub-forms. It has been commonly associated with a range of methodological strategies, including biographical method, feminist methods, personal experience accounts, narrative inquiry and conscious-raising methods (Ellis and Bochner, 2000: 740; see also Church, 1995). Auto/ethnographic writing has become a feature of many journal articles, books and theses, and tends to oscillate around a number of poles of orientation: self-feeling and relations with others; comments on the broader culture and its effect on self; or deeper reflections on the research process.

Assessing auto/ethnography?

Auto/ethnography or personal narratives of research raise concerns regarding the criteria used by various audiences to pass judgement on such writing and may attract the 'charge of self-indulgence as a regulatory mechanism' in judging such work (Sparkes, 2000: 21). These questions are of increasing relevance, as the reporting of experience becomes more a feature of research writing. Certainly, the types of assessment, encouragement or comment on auto/ethnographic writing require some discussion. Although a set of criteria may not be possible or desirable, some questions can be asked:

- To what degree should the experience be outlined?
- What experience is relevant?
- To what degree should the researcher's inner thoughts and feelings be revealed?
- How can one such researcher account be judged against another?
- What forms of expression should be given (e.g. diary, poetry, drawing, video, and so on) in the research report?
- How can these forms of expression be judged?

(Continued)

(Continued)

Here, complex methodological and epistemological issues are involved, as the forms of writing become more multitext and multivocal. These questions are likely to become more common for book, series and journal editors, who may struggle for some evaluative criteria. Sparkes reports on his own experience of positive and negative feedback from reviewers who appeared to use 'the voice of traditional science that is committed to "rationality," "objectivity," and a range of dualisms that include subject/other' (Sparkes, 2002: 193). The complexity of these issues is due to the use of different disciplinary forms of writing, which imply different 'standards' or ways of representation, 'reading' and comprehension. Again, the key question in writing about your own experience needs to be considered: 'How are others to assess your research narrative?' The notion of 'objectivity', while it can be questioned, is in fact a very powerful notion across the social science disciplines and is supported by institutional procedures (e.g. in funding, such as in social policy research initiatives).

Although closely associated with qualitative research, the 'remit' of auto/ethnography can be broadened. While often part of discussions of multiple methods involved in fieldwork research, the researcher's 'view' can be included in various types of interviewing, fact gathering, and even in the use of survey questionnaires. Some reflection and the insertion of research experience into interpretation and writing can be part of all research – both take place, affect research, and can aid the evaluation of studies.

A research text can be seen, to some extent, as 'autobiographical' in terms of the researcher's account of his or her activity. It can also be described as 'biographical' to the extent that it is reporting on the lives of others. Stanley (1993) applies the term 'auto/biography' to explore the relation between these distinctive writing practices or 'genres'. In this view, autobiography and biography are not mutually exclusive categories but are intertwined. In using the term 'auto/biography' she is drawing attention to the similarities of construction of both autobiography and biography, and how individuals are to be understood within a social milieu. The starting point of her discussion is Merton's notion of the 'sociological autobiography', which employs sociological concepts and procedures to construct a text which puts one's own life within the immediate and wider society. She then moves on to feminist sociology, with its reflexive understanding of links between the personal and political, the individual and social. By critical analytical work we can make ourselves the objects of attention. Stanley argues that conventional (non-social scientific) life-writing is usually classified according to 'naturally occurring forms' (e.g. the division between 'self' and 'society' or 'self' and 'other'). The auto/biographical approach disputes these divisions (see also Stanley, 1992).

Testimonio

Much interest has surrounded types of *'testimonio'* (or testimony) of the researched concerning their social situation and experience, for instance, of political repression, or social deprivation and discrimination (see Tedlock, 2000):

A *testimonio* is a novel or novella-length narrative, produced in the form of a printed text, told in the first person by a narrator who is also the real protagonist or witness of the events she or he recounts. Its unit of narration is usually a 'life' or a significant life experience. Because in many cases the direct narrator is someone who is either functionally illiterate or, if literate, not a professional writer, the production of a *testimonio* generally involves the tape-recording and then the transcription and editing of an oral account by an interlocutor who is a journalist, ethnographer, or literary author. (Beverley, 2000: 556)

For Beverley, similar to 'autobiography, *testimonio* is an affirmation of the authority of personal experience, but, unlike autobiography, it cannot affirm a self-identity that is separate from the subaltern group or class situation that it narrates' (Beverley, 2000: 555–6). The researcher's experience here is one of a participatory-witness to the testimony of the oppressed as well as one of mediating the story of individuals in a group to the wider audience with the objective of change.

Anthropology has been one discipline that has given much consideration to the 'voice' or 'self-life' of the researcher in the conduct and setting of the study. The starting point has been the questioning of the authority (authoricity) of the fieldworker. In traditional research:

[i]n the construction of the final ethnography, not only are the voices of many others concealed, but also that of the author. The occasional 'I' inserted in the text gives ... authorial authority but masks the intellectual and experiential biography of the ethnographer. (Okely and Callaway, 1992: xi)

For Okely, an anthropologist, the past of the researcher has to be brought into consideration but it is only relevant to the extent to which it bears upon the practice of choosing the area of study, relations in the field, and the analysis and writing of the account (Okely, 1992: 1). She argues that there has been reluctance in British anthropology to see the researcher's autobiography as an important intellectual issue. Her intent is to demonstrate the relevance of the anthropologist's past and experience in the field – the process of ethnography as mediated by sets of relationships. Not only is the biography of the researcher important in these relations but so is the experience of those studied:

> … those on the margins may first learn through an alternative personal experience their lack of fit with the dominant system. Their individual experience belies the public description at the centre. Out of their experience have arisen alternative forms on the margins. Autobiographies from the marginalised and the powerless – those of a subordinate race, religion, sex and class – have not inevitably been a celebration of uniqueness, let alone public achievement, but a record of questions and of subversion. (Okely, 1992: 7)

The notion of the autobiographical life of the researcher places him or her as very much part of the context (whether engaged in ethnographical, interview, or other relations), and changes the researcher-subject relationship as found in traditional practice:

> The autobiographical insertion is different from the stamp of author's authority: not simply 'I was there', but the self and category whom the others confronted, received and confided in. The people in the field relate to the ethnographer as both individual and cultural category, whether or not the ethnographer acknowledges this. Autobiographical accounts of fieldwork are not confined to self-understanding in a cultural vacuum. They show how others related to the anthropologist and convey the ethnographic context. (Okely, 1992: 24)

The researcher account and 'confessions'

Increasing attention has been paid in the analysis, interpretation and dissemination of research to providing a 'reflexive account' (Oliver, 2004: 25). A reflexive account enables the reader of the thesis, book, article, or research report to have some insight into the factors that have shaped the particular research process, including the writing up of the research. Further, as Oliver outlines:

> There may be an account of the courses of study they have undertaken, and mention of the institutions where they have been students. Books which the researcher has found particularly helpful or informative may be mentioned, along with conferences attended or countries visited. If relevant, the   researcher may also choose to include

mention of such issues as the influence of family or friends, various aspects of employment, or the influence of spare-time activities. In short, the reflexive account is an opportunity to outline the personal and subjective perspectives which the researcher brings to the data collection and analysis process. (Oliver, 2004: 25)

The reflection on self-identity and the research process can take a number of written forms. For example, feminist research has emphasised the importance of recognising the researcher's role, perspective and reflections on research relations and has used very detailed autobiographical reports or, more limitedly, an additional section or commentary outlining experience, reasons and feelings (Reinharz, 1992: 259). Much of these forms of writing – the confession, witness, advocacy, and so on – would be an admission of 'bias' according to a traditional or positivistic view (see Sparkes, 2002; Van Maanen, 1988). They are contrary to the accepted view of the researcher as a distanced, neutral observer-collector of 'facts' and so inconsistent with formal, rigorous research procedures and principles. But, in feminist studies, for instance, such statements are an explanation of the researcher's standpoint. Interestingly, Reinharz says that a 'norm' has 'developed that when a researcher does not live up to the standard, she atones with an apology in the publication itself'. Thus, where research is produced that is 'inadequately diversified with regard to race, age, ethnicity, and sexual preference', it has been taken as having a 'methodological weakness and moral failure, an impermissible reflection of a lack of effort and unwitting prejudice' (Reinharz, 1992: 255). Such a response may well create a range of personal difficulties for the researcher in defending or amending what he or she has reported. The motivations and omissions associated with a research study may well be questioned, and the approach taken deemed as limited, but there still remain questions concerning how far a diverse and multi-voice approach is attainable and how can it be judged (Reinharz, 1992: 258).

Self-disclosure in the text

One area of subjective experience in research that is not usually discussed is 'self-disclosure'. Routinely, as a feature of our social life, we have secrets that we may only disclose to certain others in confidence – whether colleagues or friends and relations. Some secrets we may never disclose, even to our 'nearest and dearest', especially about relationships with them. The same is true in research relations and wider academic practices. We may give something about our feelings towards others – about our research colleagues and respondents, and our department members or towards our institution itself. Such disclosures may be simply part of our views on daily circumstances, but some may have a deeper significance. Secrets and disclosures can be related to our inner uncertainties on our competence in research, or may reflect some political affiliation, sexual orientation, our health or disability, a hobby, or sporting activity that may connect with our deeper sense of self. Some areas of potential disclosure we usually wish to remain secret due to a possible loss of standing, exclusion or stigma. On the other hand, we may wish to describe some element of our 'research lives' to friends, colleagues or the respondents to show a depth of understanding, empathy or solidarity, or to legitimate and enhance our standing (for instance, as a reflective, skilled, competent or sensitive researcher).

Writing and self-identity

The process of research, including writing up, is closely related to self-identity. Ivanič (1997) says that the connection between writing and identity can be seen in four ways: the 'autobiographical self', the 'discoursal self', the 'self as author' and the 'possibilities of self-hood' (Ivanič, 1997: 24). These aspects of writer identity, we can say, can be extended to the work of the researchers in many different types of research.

The first three selves are socially constructed and socially constructing in that they are shaped by and form the more abstract 'possibilities for self-hood' which exist in the writer's socio-cultural context and 'interrelate in a that number of ways' (Ivanič, 1997: 24).

- The autobiographical self 'is the identity which people bring with them to any act of writing, shaped as it is by their prior social and discoursal history'. This self is connected to the 'writer's sense of their roots' and what they bring to writing; it 'is itself socially constructed and constantly changing as a consequence of their developing life-history; it is not some fixed, essential "real self"'.
- The discoursal self of the writer is 'the impression – often multiple, sometimes contradictory – which consciously or unconsciously conveys of themself in a particular written text'. It is 'constructed through the discourse characteristics of a text, which relate to values, beliefs and power relations in the social context in which they were written'.
- The self as author is a 'relative concept' since writers see and present themselves to varying degrees as authors. It 'concerns the writer's "voice" in the sense of the writer's position, opinions and beliefs' (Ivanič, 1997: 25–6).

These three selves or 'writer-identity' are all associated with 'actual people writing actual texts'.

- The final example is 'prototypical' 'possibilities for self-hood' (i.e. some with more privileged status than others) which are available to writers in different socio-cultural contexts and institutions (Ivanič, 1997: 27).

What we write is important to us, in how we see ourselves (e.g. as articulate, intelligent and expert) and in terms of how others regard us.

Self-monitoring

The self-monitoring of the researcher can be extended to the writing of the text itself, in a close examination of how it is written, the forms or genres applied to convince, or the 'language' employed (e.g. in the use of the first or third person). As Atkinson says, in relation to writing up ethnography:

> In the absence of any explicit frames of reference for reflexive awareness there has been a tendency, and a danger, for ethnography to be couched in textual forms that are themselves taken-for-granted. From its early years in anthropology and sociology the ethnographic monograph grew out of genres – the realist novel, the travel account, investigative journalism – that treated language relatively unproblematically. The conventions of 'realist' and 'factual' writing are themselves taken for granted. Whereas the interpretative sociologist is committed to a view of language that treats it as constitutive of reality, the ethnographic text too often seems to treat its own language as a transparent medium. There is in that a clear paradox and danger. (Atkinson, 1990: 178)

As Brewer argues, reflexivity and the writing-up process 'are inseparable'; reflexivity 'acts as a bridge between interpretation and the process by which it is conveyed in text' (Brewer, 2000: 126–7).

Writing up the research

Writing up the research document can be a very challenging process. The research material has been collected – with some relief – and now the main task of writing requires a change of direction and focus. As O'Leary reports in relation to research students:

> I have not come across many students who consider writing-up an easy or hassle-free process. Regardless of the dimension or scope of the project (your current project is likely to be your first or your biggest), writing-up is usually approached with a sense of apprehension and wariness. Well, it's no wonder when you consider that writing-up is likely to be a relatively unpractised form of writing that has major consequences attached to its quality. In fact, research is often judged not by what you did, but by your ability to report on what you did. (O'Leary, 2004: 205)

The process of research writing should be given some prior thought. For example, in what situation do you write most effectively? What tends to get in the way of writing? How much time do you have to meet any set deadlines? What outside research activities, obligations and commitments are likely to intervene? The writing up of research, although in part already prefigured by notes of various kinds, perhaps by a conference paper or journal report, entails a shift in orientation and routine. It can be a more isolated, inward process, involving long hours at the desk, that brings its particular frustrations, but it can also be a delight in expressing what you wish to say.

Setting the mood for writing

Correct body positioning in terms of an appropriate chair and desk are essential to prevent physical problems. However, the preparation for writing is more than attention to physical well-being, it also means being at 'ease' mentally. The inclination to write can very much depend on a number of factors:

- Pay attention to your working environment, especially in terms of the chair and desk used and their adjustment – correct posture, and comfortable levels of lighting and heating are very important.
- Writing can suffer numerous interruptions, for example, working at home can be subject to door-to-door sellers, phone sales, postal delivery and so on. Deal with all such distractions firmly and quickly.
- Tiredness can mean that concentration is low, perhaps due to working too hard the previous day.
- Maybe it is difficult to turn to writing after an awkward or demanding non-research project task.
- It could be that you have other things on your mind, such as a non-research, personal, domestic or work-related job (e.g. a phone call to make, a letter to write, some domestic task unfinished, a deadline approaching). If postponed, these tasks may well interfere with the writing process.
- Do not have too much clutter on or near your desk which may tempt you to 'doodle', daydream or 'play'.
- A neat organisation of materials to be used saves time from an irritating search for the right document which again can distract from the writing task.
- Have all the books, articles and notes to be used carefully arranged and to hand.
- It is advisable to keep the 'basics' in good order (i.e. the printer paper topped up and spare ink cartridges at the ready). These measures will prevent frustrations and distraction when they run out.
- When settling down, read the brief note of reminders you left after finishing writing previously.
- Try to clear your mind of other jobs and concerns.

(Continued)

- Set out what you wish to have done today, and by the end of the week.
- Relax and think positively – try to enjoy the writing.
- It tends to be the first 15 minutes or so that are needed to settle into a mental rhythm, after that writing usually begins to flow!

Often the time taken for writing up, including drafting, revising, taking comments, final version, printing, and so on, is underestimated. It may seem a period when you can hide away, put aside distraction, and complete the document smoothly. But still problems of writing up do occur. The 'simple' task of constructing an account is often much more complex than first realised, and can sometimes be delayed as a result of external personal or other demands. Writing with others can produce a much better account, but the process may have its difficulties. Individuals write in different ways and differ in how they regard deadlines. If working with someone else, make sure the 'ground rules' are clear on who is responsible for drafting different sections, their availability for discussion, the timetabling of tasks, the importance of deadlines, and so on.

Planning research writing

Planning, organisation and regularity are the watchwords of effective writing. The following tips are based on my experience of writing – as someone who used to be quite easily distracted. Others have different practices which suit them. To a certain extent each writer has to experiment to find the mode which enables him or her to write successfully.

- Try to keep to a 'normal day' if possible. If working late, have a period of relaxation before bedtime.
- Establish a clear routine. Have regular hours for writing and breaks at particular points (say, each hour) and move around. Have proper time for meals.
- Avoid time wasting. Resist frequent trips for coffee and food, newspaper reading, dealing with the post, phoning friends, etc.

(Continued)

(Continued)

- If there is a need to check emails or the internet, then this should be at a set time and for a given period. If you look at emails before writing, deal with them promptly. Do not keep looking for new messages and avoid looking at emails during your short 'breaks'. In the writing session only look at the internet to check on sources.
- Background music (at a pleasant volume) can 'cut out' distraction and allow the mind to concentrate.
- Radio voices (e.g. phone-ins or news programmes) can be off-putting, disrupting a train of thought or stimulating some distracting emotional reaction as the mind focuses on what is being said on the radio rather than the writing that has to be done.
- Have both small goals – what can be achieved today or this week – and larger goals – 'by the end of the month x chapters will be in draft'.
- Be realistic on what can be achieved.
- Write first and edit later. Do not expect to be able to write exactly what you intend straight away.
- Re-reading, re-writing and editing are necessary. Writing is hard work and does not finish with a first draft. However, seeing your work nicely presented, fluently written and with your ideas well expressed is very rewarding.
- If writing with a colleague, work out the writing tasks carefully and timetable their completion. Seek advice and help from the colleague if you are having difficulties. Do not let frustrations with a colleague develop, and be sensitive and clear when making comments on the other's work.
- Seek help from others if necessary. However, colleagues and friends may well not be critical enough. Learn to be your own 'supportive critic'.
- 'Praise yourself' for tasks completed, do not 'blame yourself' if they are not. If a large or awkward writing task has been done, say to your self 'Well done!'
- Treat yourself if you have worked hard, and even if you have not quite completed all you wished (e.g. buy a new CD or go to see a film).
- When finishing a writing session file what you have written, make copies, clear away the books you have used. Make a note of where you have got to and what the next task is (see Ward, 2002: 78).

Remember, if you do not meet the targets you have set for a writing session, try not to become anxious. Review the tasks that were set – you have worked hard and some things, however small, have been achieved!

People work in different ways. Some prefer the more 'austere' environment of a relatively bare desk and surroundings, and like to focus on the particular writing task, working steadily and taking regular breaks. Others work in a more 'relaxed' fashion, perhaps in more concentrated bursts with irregular breaks when it feels appropriate, having a drink or eating while working, even fitting in other non-research activities with writing, according to how work is progressing. As Ward says:

> The secret is to create a work environment suitable for getting *your work* done. You may find that certain conditions are a requirement to your effectiveness, while others are optional. Successful writers certainly know how to get the best out of themselves. ... What matters is your ability to concentrate on work whatever the setting ... Alternatively, there are writers who believe that you can be more productive if you create the best possible conditions for yourself. (Ward, 2002: 79)

We all expect to be able to write well and we have spent many years in education conducting various kinds of writing. However, even experienced researchers writing up their research have doubts about their ability to write effectively and with a good style. Unfortunately, we are reluctant to admit to writing difficulties – such disclosures, we feel, may lead others to question our professional abilities (Kleinman and Copp, 1993: 26).

Writing blockages

Blockages in research can take various forms, for example, those within the researcher's 'control' – 'personal blockages' (e.g. writing blockages) – and those that are not – 'external blockages' (e.g. administrative problems, perhaps to do with the release of funding, time involved in gaining ethical approval, or even transport, postage or other problems). Personal blockages can arise, due to delaying decisions in case the wrong choice is made, or due to some non-work factor (e.g. health or family) which may intrude. The term 'blockage' is probably too strong – usually it is a very temporary situation which is not a major issue. By building up confidence and energy a little, most concerns can soon be overcome and more or less forgotten.

Writing blockages

Writer's block can be defined as a pause or larger break in writing due to one or more factors. Ward gives a number of reasons for this problem:

- The material gathered is large and not as well organised as anticipated.
- It is difficult to decide on the structure and content of the document.

(Continued)

(Continued)

- It is difficult to find the right 'style'.
- There is a problem in sorting out what is important and what is not.
- Doubts arise about writing competence.
- The possible reactions to the document are too much in mind.
- There are too many outside distractions.
- Commitment is flagging, tiredness is setting in (see Ward, 2002: 96–100).

Of course, it is possible that more than one of these factors could be affecting the writing process at any given moment. Everyone has some 'blockage' at some point (an 'off day'), but usually this disruption should not last for long. When writing is going well, then there is a sense of exhilaration. Sometimes too many thoughts and ideas come 'spilling out' and have to be controlled (edited, put to one side, fashioned) according to what is required for the particular chapter or section, article or report.

Remember, you may not be quite in the mood to write, so here is some additional advice:

- If you are having difficulty writing and concentrating, write the simple, easy 'stuff' first, so that you 'write your way into' a rhythm. Perhaps some small corrections can be made, or a couple of sources can be added to the reference list?
- Writing is a series of small steps. Break your writing blocks up into smaller segments (e.g. chapters, pages or paragraphs).
- Everyone finds that sometimes it is easier to write, and there are 'bursts' of writing and 'inspiration'. Even if you are having difficulties writing, try to aim for a consistency of effort.

In trying to overcome writing blockages, think of yourself as a 'writer'. Remembering your own previous experiences may help you understand the pleasures you can have from writing, but they can also bring an awareness of earlier negative feelings and writing problems. Although the joys and sorrows of your own past experiences with writing are undoubtedly unique, there are commonalties in personal development and similarities in educational structures that typically influence the way most of us learn to write. So, looking back on our 'writing history' is an exercise in reappraising what strengths and weaknesses we have had in writing and then going on to take these into account when writing again. Rudestam and Newton (1992) argue that in the schooling system, and later, we are trained to keep our 'self' out of the writing. The link between our sense of self and what we write becomes 'distanced' and the 'pleasure' of writing is lessened. We may feel so 'stupid and unskilled' that we are put off writing altogether. They counsel that we should not despair, but nevertheless we need to overcome 'fear', 'boredom', 'perfectionism', 'disenfranchisement from your own voice', 'impatience' and 'excessive pride' that our writing is 'wonderful' (Rudestam and Newton, 1992: 149, 150–1).

Writing, writing ...

Writing regularly and having a routine are starting points, but having a clear aim for your writing is essential. What are you trying to say? What is the thread you are trying to give? Is there too much material indicated, too many theories described and too little summary?

- In writing, you need to edit your thoughts by planning.
- You will develop a better style by re-reading and rewriting, and making closer connections in your argument. The resulting work will become easier to follow and more pleasant to read.
- Writing is a laborious process but it also gives enjoyment and a sense of achievement.
- The more you write the greater your confidence and proficiency. Even established writers have to work hard on organisation, expression and style to convince others.
- It is easier to write on a subject that interests you. Being inspired by your research will keep you going despite the experience of boredom and tedium.
- In research writing, describing the research process or outlining the findings may not be as stimulating as the interpretation sections. But the basic outlines of the research are the essential foundations that enable the interpretation to be written and fully understood.

Your commitment to the subject and your intention to pass on the findings of your research will carry you through to the completion of the research writing. As Rudestam and Newton say:

Passion not only provides energy that will propel your writing project onward, but it also helps guarantee that you will interact with the materials you are writing about, testing the ideas and information of others against your own thoughts and ideas and experiences. ... Your evident investment in your topic will almost inevitably make what you write interesting to others. (Rudestam and Newton, 1992: 156)

Pressures to complete writing

There are various 'pressures' that may be associated with the writing up process:

- There may be another research project starting.
- The deadline to finish is approaching.
- Funds are running low.
- There may be a need to find a permanent job rather than 'exist' on research contracts.
- The research has become less enjoyable as the deadline approaches.
- Family and friends want more time with you or family tasks have been put off.
- The need to feel fulfilled, having overcome previous educational or career disappointments.
- The completion of the research is important for your academic or other career.
- The completion of the research will bring a feeling of success and boost confidence to meet further challenges.
- The feeling that you have spent too long on one major task – even though it is an important one.
- Others have completed or are completing their research.
- Institutional and colleagues' expectations.

In writing activities there can be shifts in emotion or mood, according to how the writer feels 'progress' is being made. Also, even 'where emotions are not part of the task itself, feelings always intrude into the flow of awareness, affecting your mood and attitude' (Layder, 2004: 25). The emotional 'strings' which appear while we are writing may originate in the social relationships and the 'interchange of emotional attitudes and dispositions' we formed during the research process, with respondents, colleagues and others since (Layder, 2004: 25).

Writing for an audience

The consideration of the nature of the intended audience, its expectations and likely receptivity, is important so that the document is comprehensible and appropriate. Who the finished piece is intended for will affect the length of document, the writing style, the layout and general organisation, and content. After finishing the research in terms of data gathering and drawing conclusions, it can seem that the research is complete. There is a wish to end the research process. However, inevitably, there is the 'writing up' to be done, putting the research 'in order', or rather 'forming' an account for an audience. The thought of writing one or more articles and trying to convince a journal that they are important enough to be published, or writing and delivering a conference paper, or relaying written feedback to research informants, can feel very daunting, after all the previous effort of research activities. Reporting to a funding body highlighting useful findings and money well spent, or writing a 70,000-word book can be even more challenging! The process of describing the research and making its findings known entails a change in orientation towards 'communication' with outside others. This is after a long period of immersion in the routines and challenges of gathering and analysing statistical information, conducting interviews, or examining documents or other materials. There may be some inner resistance to the next step in the research process, with apprehension about the worth of the study and its possible reception. However, the writer should think positively – the research has interest, and possible importance, which needs to be communicated.

Writing for an audience

In conducting research there is inevitably some anticipation of the readership and their likely assessment. Some conception of the readership or types of audience is necessary for the communication of the research to be successful, that is reaching those it is intended to and being understandable. So some anticipation of the character, orientation and knowledge of the audience is required to meet any potential difficulties in understanding the research and making its relevance clear. As Rudestam and Newton say:

> Imagining the needs and interpretive skills of your reader is a way to provide yourself with critical feedback necessary to make sure that your writing communicates what you want to say in the clearest possible fashion. Writing with this kind of awareness of your potential readers is also a good way to retain the kind of liveliness and energy that often characterizes conversation. (Rudestam and Newton, 1992: 160)

Key points to remember on researcher experience: writing up research

A number of general points need to be borne in mind when writing up research:

- Writing about research is not an emotionally detached experience and is not simply a separate research phase (i.e. found only in 'writing up').
- The researcher is also an author – before, during and after the process of 'data collection'.
- Writing is part of the construction of the 'research' – it attempts to 'represent' what has taken place.

- Academic writing has a traditional practice and form in which the researcher was a covert 'presence'.
- Writing up research includes a range of genres (e.g. description, dialogue).
- Research writing can be a contemporary commentary on research activities (e.g. in-field note-taking).
- Writing is in part an expression of the self and is affected by past writing experiences.
- Writing with others can be a rewarding experience and enhance the final product, but it can also be irritating. Individuals work at a different pace and in a different manner.
- Writing includes the anticipation of future audiences and their reactions.
- Writing up research, for many, should recognise multiple 'voices' in the text, and also a realisation that research can be written in various forms (e.g. as performance (as a play), as fiction (as a story or a blend of fact and fiction), or in a combination of forms.
- Writing requires preparation, organisation, and a 'comfortable' situation to be effective.
- Writing blockages are to some extent to be expected but can be overcome.

Summary

The process of writing has its mentally and physically demanding aspects and, if not carried out with others, can be lonely experience. While writing up should be tailored to relevant audiences in terms of being understandable and appropriate, the reaction of an audience to the finished document is still to come and cannot be fully predicted. Writing is a personal experience. The writer gives a great deal of him or herself in what is written – and a future career can often be affected by successful writing. By trial and error each writer has to find his or her own 'best practice' in writing. But, in general terms, the researcher in writing up the study should have few distractions. While writing requires a great deal of time and effort, good organisation of materials, routine, and a pleasant, supportive working environment can ease the burden. Even so, it is interesting to see the varied means by which writers 'write':

Barbara Cartland has dictated novels from a sofa, a white fur rug over her legs, a hot water bottle at her feet, two dogs beside her and a secretary with shorthand notebook at the ready. Robert Graves and Ernest Hemingway wrote while standing up. Truman Capote's favoured position was lying on a bed with a typewriter on his knees. Nick Virgilio, an American poet, sometimes writes while standing on his head because he believes he has 15 per cent more brain power when blood is rushing to the brain. What works for you? (Ward, 2002: 79)

Finally, while taking a great deal of effort, writing can also be enjoyable and satisfying – a finished report, article or book, well received, gives a 'lift' to confidence and a sense of self-worth.

Further reading

There are a number of detailed guides to research writing in general and for theses, for example, see H. Becker (1986) *Writing for Social Scientists: How to Start and Finish your Thesis, Book, or Article* (Chicago: University of Chicago Press); P. Oliver (2004) *Writing Your Thesis* (London: Sage); S.M. Coley and C.A. Scheinberg (2000) *Proposal Writing* (London: Sage); P. Crème and M.R. Lea (1997) *Writing at University* (Buckingham: Open University Press); P. Dunleavy (2003) *Authoring a PhD: How to Plan, Draft, Write and Finish a Doctoral Thesis or Dissertation* (Basingstoke: Palgrave Macmillan); M.R. Lea and B. Stierer (eds) (2000) *Student Writing in Higher Education* (Buckingham: SRHE and Open University Press); D. Silverman (2000) *Doing Qualitative Research: A Practical Handbook* (London: Sage), Part 5; A. Thody (2006) *Writing and Presenting Research* (London: Sage); and A. Ward (2002) 'The writing process', in S. Potter (ed.), *Doing Postgraduate Research* (London: Sage). More specifically for qualitative research, see A. Holliday (2001) *Doing and Writing Qualitative Research* (London: Sage), which has substantial discussions on writing about data, the writer's voice and writing about research relations. On use of relevant literature, see C. Hart (2001) *Doing a Literature Search* (London: Sage) and C. Hart (1998) *Doing a Literature Review* (London: Sage). For connections between writing and argument see G.J. Fairbairn and C. Winch (1991) *Reading, Writing and Reasoning: A Guide for Students* (Buckingham: Open University Press). For a discussion of the importance of writing in relation to identity, see R. Ivanič (1997) *Writing and Identity* (Amsterdam: John Benjamins). For excellent reviews of auto/ethnography and *testimonio*, see A.C. Sparkes (2002) *Telling Tales in Sport and Physical Activity: A Qualitative Journey* (Leeds: Human Kinetics), Chapter 5; C. Ellis and A.P. Bochner (2000) 'Autoethnography, personal narrative, reflexivity' and J. Beverley (2000) 'Testimonio, subalternity, and narrative authority', both in N.K. Denzin and Y.S. Lincoln (eds) (2000) *Handbook of Qualitative Research* (2nd edn, London: Sage).

7

DISSEMINATION

The postmodernist position is deeply unsettling about the publications that we read and the research on which they are based. (Becker and Bryman, 2004: 363)
    We are writing for our lives, and for the lives of others as well, for our words matter. … The sociologist's voice must speak to the terrible and magnificent world of human experience in the first years of the 21st century. (Denzin, 2001: 155)

What is 'research dissemination'?

Researchers have an obligation to make their study known to others, and a funding body or institution will set certain requirements. If the research is regarded as important for social policy, or in terms of a sociological substantive area, and in theory and methodology employed, then the researcher has some obligation to disseminate it appropriately. Dissemination 'is concerned with the communication to relevant audiences of information and knowledge gained from research'; as such, it is 'an integral part of the policy research process' (Becker and Bryman, 2004: 361). Broadly, to disseminate means to spread, scatter around, propagate, disperse, diffuse, communicate or publicise the research findings, and the research process and methods. 'It is important' as Potter says, 'to have a clear view of the output(s) required from the earliest opportunity – at the research design stage if possible' (Potter, 2004: 371).

Potential outlets for the research work can include 'oral' forms, such as merely discussing it with colleagues (or family and friends), small presentations or workshops to the department, or more formal seminars or lectures to undergraduates, or to postgraduates and staff. Conference papers or other presentations can be given about research both prior to and post publication of the final article, report or book. Additionally, especially in the social policy field, a funding organisation may well wish to give a press release or plan a special seminar or conference. Similarly, dissemination of written materials can be through various means – perhaps by email notes to colleagues, or by sending draft copies to researchers in the field for comment. Research findings may take the form of a conference abstract, distributed conference presentation notes or be published in conference proceedings. The research may form the basis of one or more articles (or research notes) for journals, a book or a report. Joining a research interest group is a good way of disseminating ideas and research interests. Dissemination through publication may also be to a very wide audience, possibly through an article or being interviewed for a popular magazine or local or national newspaper. Information may also be placed on the Web and be made available for a discussion group or on open access.

To describe the process of dissemination as taking place through 'outlets' would make it seem like a one-way process, merely delivering the research findings to an audience. In fact, it is a more interactive phenomenon: the receipt of comments from participants, sponsors and others may be an important influence prior to 'formal' dissemination. Conference papers or other presentations are usually followed by questions from the audience and these may 'feed' into subsequent forms of dissemination. Also, books and articles receive responses from editors and publishers' reviewers prior to publication, while later book reviews or article comments are part of the ongoing dialogue on the research. The study may be disseminated further by comments and evaluations made by authors in their books, articles or reports.

Dissemination outlets

The outlets for research are very diverse and can include both academic and non-academic dissemination, and can be oral, written or performed – or a combination of these, for example reading a paper to non-academic professionals.

(Continued)

(Continued)

Oral presentations and papers

- Informal discussion with colleagues within your institution.
- Lecture, seminar or research workshop in undergraduate or postgraduate teaching.
- Lecture, seminar or research workshop to departmental colleagues.
- Lecture, seminar or research workshop at another academic institution.
- Informal discussion or seminars with other researchers in the field.
- Presentations to outside bodies (e.g. professionals, client groups, campaigning organisations) relevant to your research subject.
- Conference papers to professional organisations or a more specialist research grouping.
- Presentation to a funding body and/or the researched institution.
- Presentation to research respondents/informants.

Written works

- Conference paper abstract.
- Journal article or research report.
- Book article.
- Book.
- Research report to funding body.
- Press release (e.g. by funding body).
- Report or interview in the media (newspaper, magazine, radio, television).
- Research summary to the researched group or organisation.
- Video, CD, web page, email discussion group.
- A combination of several of the above outlets.

Dissemination and audience issues

Commonly, dissemination is seen as a particular stage in the research process after a '*cognitive phase* and the *doing research phase*', all of which 'need to be managed effectively' if the research is to be considered 'rigorous' and the findings 'trustworthy' (Becker and Bryman, 2004: 362). However, while dissemination takes place mainly following the 'final' writing up, dissemination, as mentioned earlier, can occur throughout the research, even at the start before the survey, interviews or fieldwork have been undertaken and the first statistical test or interpretation carried out. For example, the intention to research on a particular topic and in a certain way may be relayed to others in various ways possibly to gain responses which may help frame the intended research further.

Principles of research dissemination

Becker and Bryman (2004) argue that it is important for researchers to discuss a study with funders and other intended audiences for the research, for instance, 'policy makers, politicians, practitioners, users of services, research funders, other researchers and academics, and potentially, the public as a whole'. They also advise that specific audiences may wish to know about different parts of the research and the findings (Becker and Bryman, 2004: 361–2).

Dissemination of research to a studied community

Colin Bell (1977) 'Reflections on the Banbury Restudy', in C. Bell and H. Newby (eds), *Doing Sociological Research*. London: George Allen and Unwin.

Bell interestingly describes how the activities of a community restudy were disseminated to the town concerned:

> We had always planned to have a public meeting to 'tell' Banbury that we were there and what we were up to. This was greeted by the *Oxford Mail* with the headline 'New Probe Into "Snob Town"'. Most of the press coverage we received, though, was considerably more helpful and enthusiastic. We felt that through this public meeting and through the local press we were going some way towards meeting the Nuffield Foundation's [the funding body] request. Our meeting was eventually held in March 1967, in the Town Hall, and was chaired by the Mayor. It was attended by about 100 people, including half the Borough Council and many of Margaret Stacey's [the author of the original study] old acquaintances. The audience was swollen by some of the ladies we had already recruited to interview for us and members of an adult education class I was running in the town. Bill Williams [Bell's PhD supervisor] and Margaret Stacey came up from Swansea for the meeting, and they and I spoke from the platform. (Bell, 1977: 58; see also Stacey, 1960, and Stacey et al., 1975)

This is an instance of a formal presentation that is open to a community as a whole. More usually, individual respondents or a small group of those involved in a piece of research are contacted, and part of the research is given to them to read and respond to.

A number of issues arise when the publication of research is being considered, involving the choice of the type of outlet, what obligations are owed to funding bodies, the intended audience, the appropriate style and structure of reportage, and ethical concerns relating to those researched. For example, as Potter (2004) asks, who 'owns' the research and is responsible for dissemination? He adds that there are costs and benefits of the 'dissemination strategy' adopted, and consideration should be given to them when dissemination takes place. Further issues concern the extent to which the research participants should be informed about the findings, whether the media should be used in dissemination and whether the aim of dissemination is to influence policy (Potter, 2004: 371–8). A general obligation to the researched is 'to do no harm' and to have possible benefit to their lives. This is a vexed area since the research may bring to light crimes or misdemeanours, or information about an oppressed group whose wider dissemination may not help their 'cause'.

The British Sociological Association (BSA) provides a number of obligations that a researcher has towards funders or sponsors, including informing them of changes in the character of the research and that appropriate time is available to report. It also says that the researcher should be open to the observations made by participants and the sponsors/funders, and be committed to disseminate research findings while 'normally' resisting attempts to curtail the freedom to spread research conclusions (see Seale, 2004). The BSA declares that there is a relationship between the sociologist and sponsor/funder which should be based on the pursuit of objective inquiry and in a way that provides for suitably high professional standards – to obtain appropriate information and resist any pressure towards certain results and outcomes. However, sociologists should be clear that although they have obligations to funders, they also have obligations to their participants, colleagues and research community as well as the wider society. Researchers therefore have to be aware of the interests of various audiences involved and affected by the research.

The doctoral thesis

The traditional expectation of the doctoral thesis (in the UK) was that once it was completed and awarded one or two copies were formally placed in the university library and there it would stay probably untouched, despite the usual injunction that the PhD should be of 'publishable standard'. However, there is increasing pressure to publish doctoral work (even before the thesis is finished) by adapting the thesis into a published book or series of articles. In the UK the doctoral 'process' includes a viva with up to three examiners (possibly two of whom are external to the university and one internal as chair). The main supervisor of the doctoral student may be present as an observer. The examiners will have read the thesis and perhaps given an initial report to the university prior to the viva, for instance, on main areas to be covered in questions to the student. The thesis may well be read by a reviewer in the university before formal submission to see if it conforms to university format and regulations and for a general checking over (e.g. whether the contents page conforms to the body of the text, whether the references are complete, etc.). The whole process in the UK has become more detailed and clearer to the student than perhaps twenty years ago. In many parts of the rest of Europe the viva is a more substantial occasion; the student has to defend the thesis in public (a mainly invited audience in a lecture theatre) with an appointed discussant giving a general view and asking various questions to which the student responds. There is also an examining panel in the audience.

The viva

The viva can be considered as a particular form of dissemination. Some anxiety at the prospect of a viva is normal and understandable. It can be lessened by remembering that you have sought and taken advice from your supervisors; also that the viva should allow you to demonstrate an awareness of the particular issues and give a coherent explanation. Following the viva, it is highly likely that the examining committee will ask for some changes to the text before the dissertation is accepted, the smallest amendment usually being the correction of typographical slips and minor errors in some references. The examiners will often provide a list of such changes for you and your supervisor. More extensively, there might also be some editing, additions and possibly some clarifications required, which usually can be done quite quickly (e.g. in methodology), and then final approval of the thesis is given. A return to the thesis to make careful changes and corrections is obviously necessary. Although a tedious and frustrating process, the reward of completion is worth the additional effort! (see Silverman, 2000: Chapter 22)

The research report and briefing

Research reports and briefings are often in a particular format, with clear subheadings and numbered findings or recommendations. A research or sponsoring body will probably provide guidelines for the format needed, and previous reports may well be a good guide. Briefings are often given to representatives of the sponsors or the research committee that has overseen the research study, particularly if it involves a substantial amount of funding. Such bodies may require some public briefing using the media – a press release, a press conference, or a media interview. In such cases, the sponsoring body will be involved; it will give advice and will have its own procedures for media involvement. Contact with the media can be an intimidating prospect, so it is advisable to take some training, at least some advice, on how to act in a radio or television interview. Universities have a press office and the researcher should seek its advice when dealing with the media, especially if the research is likely to create a great deal of public interest. The university may wish to circulate the findings internally and even publicise the research on its own website. The researcher should also consider placing an account (usually very brief) on his or her own home page or on that of the department, again following advice from a technical administrator and others, such as guidance from the department head and university press office.

The conference paper

Conference presentations can be of different durations, ranging from perhaps only ten minutes, to more often twenty minutes, with about five minutes allowed for questions from the audience. A call for conference papers some months before the conference is usual, requesting an abstract which will often be refereed. Then, hopefully, the proposed paper will be accepted. The size of audience for a conference paper will vary. Usually around 15 people could be expected to hear a paper, with about three other presenters and a chair who introduces the session. If you are making a presentation, it is advisable to go to an earlier session to see the layout and likely size and type of audience, and to check that the technology requested is available and works. Just in case there are problems with the technology, you should be ready to present without it and also to be able to give a shortened version of your paper if for some reason you have less time than was allotted. If you know what to expect, you should feel more confident. Those chairing sessions tend to differ in strictness of timekeeping and some speakers are difficult to stop! But, if you have a strategy to reduce the length of your paper if time is shorter than expected or to expand a little if you have gone too quickly, then you will feel well prepared for likely problems of timing.

Giving a conference paper

Presenting a conference paper or giving a talk in some other forum should be an enjoyable and useful experience. It is normal to feel some apprehension – no matter how experienced the presenter is, there are always some 'nerves'. Having given a successful paper with some interesting and supportive comments, a researcher can receive quite an emotional uplift. I remember giving a paper at an international conference, after quite a time without having presented my work. I felt quite nervous beforehand and was the last speaker out of four, one of whom was internationally renowned so the session was much more crowded (and hot and uncomfortable) than previous ones. However, having given my paper, I was relieved to receive very favourable comments and the previous anxieties were forgotten. I learned a great deal about presenting and my own personal abilities and emotional resources from that occasion.

Listed below are some guidelines for presenting a conference paper.

- If you are inexperienced, practise giving your paper and receiving questions with a small group and gain feedback.
- Ideally you should be able to reduce a presentation to a number of headings, and a number of passages, but have the full paper with you just in case you feel less confident or have spoken too quickly. In that way you can 'fill in time' by reading a couple of extra passages.
- Everyone feels some 'nerves' before giving a paper. Breathe deeply, try to relax your body and remember other occasions when you have spoken about your work.
- Pre-check the conference room and the technology you intend to use.
- Start with a smile, and show some 'energy' – show you are interested in your topic!
- If you are to read out a great deal, look up and around at frequent intervals to aid communication, reception and interest from the audience.
- Usually conference papers are delivered standing. If inexperienced, you may feel more at ease delivering the paper seated rather than standing.
- Take care on the 'pace' of your talk. Speak clearly, introduce the main points and sections, and keep to your structure. Always leave time to conclude.
- Remember questions will be asked. It is a relief to finish a paper and you can relax a little, but do not forget questions are to follow.
- In some sessions audience questions are asked after each paper, in others they are asked at the end when all the papers have been delivered.

(Continued)

(Continued)

- Listen to the question carefully. If you are not clear on what is being asked, politely ask the questioner to say it again or ask if he or she means 'this' or 'that'.
- Be careful not to respond aggressively, even if the person appears to be saying something sharply, be polite and to the point. If you feel the questioner is making a good point, say so, even if you do not fully agree.
- Many questioners can be very helpful in stating something you had not quite seen in your research, or suggesting sources and further developments, or relating your work to their own research.
- Having finished your talk and answered the questions, relax and enjoy the rest of the conference!
- If an inexperienced presenter, your confidence will have risen and you will feel more able to ask questions of other presenters, discuss topics between sessions with others and feel more able to 'socialise' generally.
- Frequently, it is said that the 'out-of-session' discussions are just as valuable as paper sessions.

It is often in conference and other similar sessions that researchers feel more able to 'reveal' their research experiences. Moch describes 'talking' about research experience at conferences and asks why this information is less acceptable for publications:

We have frequently wondered why talking about the researcher experience is acceptable but writing about the experience and getting the researcher experience accepted for publication is unlikely. Not talking about the researcher experience may further exacerbate denial of the researcher experience for researchers and publishers. Maybe if the researcher is purposefully left out of the research report, the research can seem more 'objective' and 'true'. (Moch, 2000b: 127)

Articles in books and journals

Submitting an article to a journal and receiving its decision can be a long process and can end in the disappointment of a rejection letter from an editor. Even very experienced academics with a long publication record may have to face being turned down by a journal. At the same time there is increasing pressure from departments, at least in the UK, to publish in highly rated national and international journals. Due to the national Research Assessment Exercise in the UK, subject groups at institutions are nationally rated and money is 'won' from a central body if a high grade is achieved. Staff who do not publish or whose publications do not fit the subject area, or whose publications are not deemed to be of sufficient worth, are excluded from the process. In this way, the distinction between those who 'publish' and those who 'teach' is becoming more established.

Getting your article published in a journal

For a new researcher or new academic it is not always easy to find or decide on the journal that might be most suitable for an article. Even for the more experienced researcher, the increase in numbers of journals means they may not be sure of the appropriate outlet. In short, the writer has to do some 'research' to find the relevant journals, by asking colleagues, searching in the library, using internet sources, consulting publishers' catalogues or noting journals that are used by key writers in the field.

There are ways of increasing the possibility of your article being published:

- Get to know the journals that cover your field. A common reason for the rejection of an article is that it is not considered appropriate for the journal concerned (see Day, 1996; Silverman, 2000: 267).
- Journals provide the basic details for submission. These can often be found in the immediate inside of the journal and on its web pages. Articles are usually about 6–7,000 words in length.
- A journal may also include shorter pieces, such as a commentary on a previous article, a brief research report, a review of research on a given area, book reviews, or a small debating piece. Submitting a short piece such as these will give you practice and confidence in writing.
- Examine carefully previously published pieces in a relevant journal. Note the style, expression, degree of referencing and also what topics or issues are featured or are likely to be of interest, for example, a further 'twist' to a current debate or an additional research contribution.
- A close examination of several articles submitted to the journal you have chosen will give you a good idea of the acceptable format. For example, take a good look at the abstract, aims and introduction, review of previous literature (studies, theories and issues), the research and its findings, implications for the subject area, conclusion, notes and references.
- Remember that a journal article is different from a chapter in a thesis or book. By reading previous articles, an indication of how to frame an article based on your research should become clear.
- Make sure that your research is placed in the context of other work and that you do not try to present too much data and theorisation. Identify

(Continued)

(Continued)

the relevant issues, give your aim(s) clearly and how your research and approach differs from others, keep a central theme or argument, and conclude clearly, summarising your contribution.

- Having written the piece, check it very carefully several times for errors and format (e.g. are the references listed in the required manner?). Errors are irritating for the journal reviewers to read.
- If the article is in the chosen journal's format and is well presented, it shows a degree of care and serious intent to the editor, and that less detailed editing will be necessary if the article is accepted.

Before submitting an article, eliciting a response from other colleagues to the piece can be useful. However, the readers you ask may not be critical enough or give only general feedback. Silverman says that an article is more likely to be published if it has a clear focus, avoids unnecessary detail, improves discussion and understanding, and keeps in mind the audience to be addressed (which will be different, say, from your PhD examiners or a sponsor) (Silverman, 2000; Chapter 23). If the article is not rejected, a provisional acceptance will be based on referees' comments, which will have to be taken into account according to the editor's direction. Changes can range from minor corrections in wording and references to more substantial alterations in content (e.g. such as making the central argument clearer, including some further literature, or reducing or reordering some material). In general, it is important to gain the interest of the readers of a journal or book article, and establish the relevance of the research in relation to previous work or an ongoing debate in a field (Silverman, 2000: 267; see also Czarniawska, 2004: 118).

Books – proposals and publishers

There are two main types of initial contact with a publisher: first, by sending an outline directly; and secondly, by being approached by a publisher, usually by a series editor (often another academic), to ask if you would consider writing a text. In both cases a detailed proposal will have to be written to be approved by the publisher. This may involve sending the proposal to other academics for a review and a recommendation. If the publisher is interested in the proposal, they may well send a number of queries based on the proposal guidelines. If accepted, a standard contract will then be issued for the writer to sign. This will include a deadline and perhaps a small sum as an advance on future royalties. It is usually not a good idea to send a completed PhD thesis or research report to a publisher as these are intended for particular audiences and it is unlikely that they will be sent to other academics for review or receive a positive response. A number of preliminary steps are necessary to try to avoid the disappointment of a (sometimes fairly swift) rejection, which will come as quite a blow following the successful completion of a thesis or research work. The key words here are preparation and presentation. Some research on likely publishers is necessary to find out which ones publish in the particular field or are expanding in that area, and the series editor to contact.

Detailed examination of the publisher's catalogue, which can often be accessed from or ordered via the Web, will give the publisher's current interests. It is also worth examining closely the required length of the books in a particular series (70,000 words is common), how the series is described, how many chapters are usual, the specific books within the series, what are the intended audiences (undergraduate, postgraduate, or general reader), and what is the style or format. It might also help to obtain a couple of the books in the series to see more closely the type of book that is published and the format that is required. For example, as a researcher, your book will be based on a social investigation that has been carried out, and will not be a textbook which introduces a field. So, you will need to find a publisher's series relevant to your research area. The would-be author should see not only if the proposed book is likely to fit into the requirements of a series, but also, importantly, if there is a 'gap' which it could fill. Note here that a publisher will also often advertise forthcoming books. In this way, you are focusing on a likely publisher, and considering carefully how your study can be adapted as a book for a particular series, rather than sending the proposal 'cold'. It may be, on further thought, that you prefer a different audience, aim, format, book length and so on than the particular series considered.

Submitting a book proposal

It is important to present a book idea well using the publisher's guidelines.

- A good outline of what is intended (e.g. detailed rationale, chapter summaries) is necessary so that the publisher can make an informed judgement on content and competing texts.
- A good outline is also a very good guide for when you write the book since you have already made and thought through a detailed plan.

(Continued)

(Continued)

- Care is needed in describing a proposed book. Publishers and retailers like to have a 'market focus' so that it can be readily categorised, given a place in their catalogues, and publicised appropriately (e.g. by sending it to particular journals or exhibiting it at specialist conferences).
- The proposal should be clearly written, professionally presented, and should demonstrate the appeal of the research, what is distinctive, and what it adds to the intended series.

Books give more scope for the inclusion of the researcher's experience of research and a description of what happened – research activities, procedures, events and relationships affecting the research process. For Moch: 'To publish in book form, authors need not convince traditional peer reviewers that the researcher experience is important to the research report. Through book form, authors have the liberty and often the space to share the researcher experience' (Moch, 2000b: 128).

The internet

University departmental and research centre web pages are an invaluable means of publicising research and publications. This information can lead to contacts from book series editors, other researchers, and PhD and other research students. The internet can be considered as a 'research context' (see Markham, 2004). It eases collaboration in writing (e.g. the sending of drafts between co-writers who are very far apart) and general debate with others in the same field. Researchers are increasingly using web groups to exchange information (e.g. through electronic journals, discussion groups and email), including the reporting of ongoing research. Thus, it is possible to take advice, share information, 'disseminate' research materials and findings much more readily, in a more 'ongoing' fashion than previously.

Similarly, contact with informants or respondents in the research setting (who may be quite distant) is becoming easier over the Web, including research by text and/or video. For some researchers, 'weblogs' provide not only a new tool for the dissemination of ideas, practices and findings to an audience beyond academia, but also a new form of 'accountability' to the public. This accountability opens up new questions concerning not only the research process but also relations of the researcher to the university or funder, the researched, and this wider general audience while the research is in progress. Here are various issues regarding the confidentiality and anonymity of respondents, how and the extent to which information is shared, and the means by which 'writing up' and publication takes place.

Internet usage also affects the relationships and experience of the researcher as time and spatial shifts are further 'compressed'. Instead of research being a strictly linear set of phases, at least as described in traditional research guides, now, perhaps due to demands for research to be quicker and because of the application of new technology, the various research tasks and relations can be more coterminous, leading to 'dissemination' taking place throughout the research process.

Research and teaching – the use of research in the classroom

The practice and findings of research are also passed on in the classroom – in tutorials, seminars and lectures – and not only the 'who', 'what', 'when', 'where', 'how' and 'whys' of research, the findings, interpretative procedures and theoretical perspectives, but also research experiences and activities. Teaching can also be an excellent forum for discussion of the personal aspects of research by giving a closer picture of the satisfactions and joys, the difficulties and apprehensions. In seminars, workshops and lectures to undergraduate and postgraduate students, the implications for research experience of various styles of research, contexts and participant groups, and ethical issues, can be relayed and discussed. The researcher-as-teacher can add to textbook methodological guides a first-hand knowledge of research activity, and thereby give reassurance and confidence to students as someone who has successfully completed an investigation.

Key points to remember on researcher experience: the dissemination of research

- Dissemination begins well before the 'research' is finished. It should not be considered as a secondary 'after-thought'.
- Researcher experience is often given in informal settings (e.g. discussions with colleagues) and conferences but much less so in published work.
- There are many possible outlets for research findings and experiences.
- Being in print is an 'ego-boosting' experience as well as important for an academic career.
- Test out your ideas and findings in more informal settings, and practise giving presentations.
- Research audiences are very varied (and can be wider than the academic audience), and require different forms of dissemination.
- The PhD viva and thesis are very particular modes of presentation and communication.

- Outlets for dissemination must be carefully chosen. The article, conference paper, or other means of dissemination should be well constructed to meet the requirements of intended outlets and their audiences.
- Attention must be paid to writing and presentational style, and the extent to which it is possible to provide a reflexive account for the particular audience.
- Any use of the media as a vehicle for dissemination requires careful consideration, including liaison with funders and the researcher's own organisation on what is appropriate.

Summary

This chapter has discussed what is meant by 'dissemination', the various ways it can take place, and the audiences it is aimed at. Audiences can include funding bodies, academic audiences in the researcher's institution or at conferences, and journal and book readerships. The internet is also providing new opportunities for the dissemination of information about the researcher's experience and activities.

The dissemination of research, at least until recently, has not been considered in detail in textbooks, or given much systematic thought by researchers. In fact, dissemination is both a very important and complex part of the research process. There is increasing pressure on postgraduate students and academics to publish, and the issue of dissemination is gaining in significance in research texts and discussion. The dissemination of the experiences in research is becoming more prevalent but its extent differs according to the form of outlet.

The dissemination of researcher experience is increasingly seen as providing insights into how a study was conducted, how information was sorted and constructed, how ideas and interpretation take place (or 'knowledge' is produced), how the research write-up is completed, and the research communicated. But, as Moch adds: 'If the researcher experience troubles us as it does, and if the researcher experience is often included in presentations at research conferences, research methods seminars, and in conversations with research colleagues, why is evidence of the researcher experience so limited in published works?' (Moch, 2000b: 127)

Further reading

On presenting research, see P. Cryer (2000) *The Research Student's Guide to Success* (Buckingham: Open University Press), Chapter 14, and for a fuller discussion, see P. McCarthy and C. Hatcher (2002) *Presentation Skills: The Essential Guide for Students* (London: Sage). More broadly on dissemination, audiences and evaluation, see: S. Becker and A. Bryman (eds) (2004) *Understanding Research for Social Policy and Practice* (Bristol: The Policy Press), Part 7; S. Brown, D. Black, A. Day and P. Race (1998) *500 Tips for Getting Published: A Guide for*

Educators, Researchers and Professionals (London: Kogan Page); A. Thody (2006) *Writing and Presenting Research* (London: Sage); A. Richardson, C. Jackson and W. Sykes (1990) *Taking Research Seriously: Means of Improving and Assessing the Use and Dissemination of Research* (London: HMSO (Department of Health)); and C. Seale et al. (eds) (2004) *Qualitative Research Practice* (London: Sage), Part 6. L. Richardson (1990) *Writing Strategies: Reaching Diverse Audiences* (London: Sage) provides a short account of theoretical and practical issues, writing academic papers and the public. More specifically on research and the media, see Economic and Social Research Council (ESRC) (1993) *Pressing Home Your Findings: Media Guidelines for ESRC Researchers* (Swindon: Economic and Social Research Council). Finally, the relations between social researchers and social policy-makers are usefully examined in M. Bloor (2004) 'Addressing social problems through qualitative research', in D. Silverman (ed.), *Qualitative Research: Theory, Method and Practice* (2nd edn, London: Sage).

8

REACTIONS TO RESEARCH

Chapter overview

Reactions to research dissemination
'Self' and audience reactions to research
Feedback on journal article submission
Key points to remember on researcher experience: dealing with reactions to research
Summary
Further reading

If alternative forms of qualitative inquiry and new writing practices are judged using inappropriate criteria, there is the danger that they will be dismissed as not being proper research and, therefore, not worthy of attention. (Sparkes, 2002: 194)

Including the researcher experience in research reporting may call into question the objectivity rule of science. Insistence on the objectivity rule in research journals may be the reason scientific journals do not include the researcher experience. (Moch, 2000b: 128)

Reactions to research dissemination

Publishing a first book or article is a personal milestone and can have a particular benefit for the researcher in terms of career. Of course, reviews or comments on published work may not be entirely favourable. However, to gain a review for a study, even if it is lukewarm, especially in a major journal, is an advantage when compared with no review at all! Good reviews can be perceived by an author as recognition of what has been achieved by all the effort put in. However, some criticism is to be expected. In fact, the more widespread the study is quoted the more detailed assessment is likely to take place alongside instances of 'misreading' and simplification. The number of times the study is cited also becomes a kind of rating of its 'importance' in the field. Needless to say, there are numerous instances of books that are commonly cited but often not read in detail, and some neglected books only in retrospect appear to be groundbreaking. Like many other fields of activity, academic publishing has its 'fashions'. It is easier to have a book published or to receive research funds in the first place on a specific area, issue or author where these are subject to rising interest and there is a favourable 'market' for dissemination.

Reaction to research can be varied and may take place at any point in the research process – not just at the end. At a very early stage, it can be in the form of feedback on the research proposal to a funding body or on a tentative formulation made to close colleagues. There can also be responses even a long time after the research has finished. Feedback of various sorts can range from the comments of co-workers, department members, and non-work individuals, to more formal responses, for instance, by an audience at a conference presentation. Referees' evaluations on submitted journal articles or the views of funders and readers of a research report, book reviews or responses to the formal presentation of findings at a special event publicising the research findings, can all be considered part of 'audience reaction'. These varied sources of feedback give very different opportunities for the researcher's own responses – welcoming the help, accepting or rejecting critical points, or taking the opportunity for some continued dialogue or debate. There are some instances when debate is not possible, for example, a direct response to anonymous comments by journal or research proposal referees.

Today, with increasing experimentation with different forms of writing and 'representation' of research, there can be some adverse reaction if writing or presentation appears to 'stray' from previously accepted conventions. Sparkes (2002) describes Richardson's experience of converting a life-history interview into a long poem, which was then delivered at a major conference. This raises again the issues of the kinds of data, criteria and the acceptance by other sociologists of unusual procedures that may transgress disciplinary boundaries or challenge assumptions (Sparkes, 2002: 197; see also Richardson, 1990). Not surprisingly, there is often resistance to new ideas surrounding writing and presentation – despite the shifts that have taken place in recent years. Where boundaries of acceptance are crossed, with the rupturing of what is commonly accepted, reactions can range from an off-hand dismissal or merely ignoring the work presented, to a fierce denunciation. A research write-up or presentation may be deemed, on the one side, as 'pioneering' or, on the other, as illegitimate in terms of what counts as appropriate portrayals of research. Of course, these reactions can include the conduct of research itself where new approaches are being explored in both methodological and representational terms.

The way we are professionally socialised forms our outlook and identity as 'sociologists' or 'sociological researchers'. Thus, to challenge key aspects of professional procedure, as in the crossing of disciplinary boundaries, is to question core beliefs, professional orientation and self-identity of others similarly socialised. There are boundaries of convention, discipline, forum or situation, which are learnt directly and indirectly within professional social-isation and sociologists come to accept these as the 'ways of doing'. On the other hand, explorations in method and representation offer exciting new ways of approaching research. New developments can bring new opportu-nities in terms of career development and research proposals can be framed and adapted to reflect emerging practices. Implicated here, in the accep-tance of shifts in practices, perspectives, writing and funding, are the hierar-chies of the discipline – the structuring of the production of research work in departments and universities, funding organisations, government agen-cies, and professional associations. These bodies can sponsor, restrict and shape the kinds of investigation that researchers in a discipline undertake.

'Self' and audience reactions to research

'Self-reactions' to research being undertaken begin right at the start of the research process when the topic for investigation is being formulated, as Bottomley, on starting his PhD found:

While I was going through these preliminary stages of sorting out a viable topic I felt inadequate, a bit flighty and scatterbrained even, because I kept changing topics. Even though I was aware that many other students doing higher degrees had been through the same hoops, the sheer weight and subtle pervasiveness of mainstream orthodoxy was such that I didn't seriously entertain the possibility that this indecisiveness on my part might stem from structural faults in the system I was working within. (Bottomley, 1978: 218)

Bottomley says that he 'would have found it encouraging if more people had supported [his] decision to research a question that [he] had become genuinely intrigued by, rather than getting that uncomfortable look in their eye and cautioning [him] to be practical'. Like many researchers he discov-ered that the 'solicitous queries' of others as to his progress only added to his 'own feeling of urgency' (Bottomley, 1978: 219). The 'self-as-audience' includes a necessary self-scrutiny – characteristics that should be part of any ongoing research practice and not simply a retrospective 'self-disclosure' (to oneself and others) at the end of research. So, questions are asked by the researcher such as: 'Am I really interested in the research?' 'Does it raise the theoretical or methodological questions that really interest me?'

Colleagues and friends in the same subject area are a source of comment and advice both on research procedures and problems, and on written work. Often such feedback may not be sufficiently evaluative, since friends and close colleagues may be reluctant to be 'critical'. But, nevertheless, it is a source of support and may provide relevant information on the detail of your work or on possible journals or book editors looking for articles on your particular topic. What other researchers and colleagues say – in positive or negative terms – has a direct effect on self-esteem and the feelings you have towards your research and role. A self-questioning arises – 'Was my research worthwhile?' 'Am I a competent researcher after all?' 'What do others now think of my research and my capabilities?'

Meeting an audience face to face leaves the researcher open to some questioning – credibility has to be achieved, the research has to be presented coherently and convincingly. As Ramazanoğlu states:

> Meeting your audience (whether in person or in print, by negotiation, invitation or in competition with others) is the point at which you make yourself vulnerable by offering your knowledge claims up to be challenged. Making this commitment can be not only politically and intellectually challenging, but also emotionally demanding. (Ramazanoğlu, 2002: 162)

Speaking of feminist researchers, she adds that it 'can be a baptism of fire to present feminist conclusions to an audience that shares none of your assumptions; it can encourage complacency only to target audiences where all your assumptions are shared'. Researchers can face challenges where they have undertaken 'unorthodox' methodologies, studied groups who are seen as unworthy by society and where societal assumptions about them are strong, or presenting findings and interpretations that go against the grain of preconceived ideas (Ramazanoğlu, 2002: 162). Nevertheless, the researcher should not be afraid of expressing some doubts, being open to other views, and welcoming responses. On the other hand, an audience may well have certain preconceptions of an investigator and his or her specific area of research. Okely found:

> To outsiders learning of my research, I was sometimes seen as a 'Gypsy woman', with all the fantastic stereotypes. Vivid and contrasting examples of actual Gypsy women from my fieldwork were recalled. ... I had not and could not have predicted the paradoxes in Gypsy women's position either before or during fieldwork. (Okely, 1994: 31–2)

Media reactions before research starts!

R.G. Hollands (2000) ' "Lager louts, tarts, and hooligans": the criminalization of young adults in a study of Newcastle night-life', in V. Jupp et al. (eds), *Doing Criminological Research*. London: Sage.

(Continued)

(Continued)

Reaction to research can take place 'early on', even before any initial findings, merely on the knowledge about a proposed study, or its first steps. Hollands describes how he was successful in gaining an Economic and Social Research Council (ESRC) award in 1993 to undertake research on youth culture and the city (Newcastle). The focus was on young people 'going out' at night during a period of important socio-economic change, shifts in forms of consumption and postponed transitions from the household. The intention was to explore the study of youth culture in relation to urban and labour market transformation. Much to his surprise, Hollands says:

> I was caught completely unawares by the level of public debate, reaction and exposure the project generated, even before it officially began. News of the grant award was first reported in both Newcastle newspapers and regional television stations, before circulating more widely by appearing as a story in eight national dailies, and on Radio 5 and BBC Northern Ireland radio. It gained international coverage in Canada, through two radio interviews with the Canadian Broadcasting Company (CBC), before finding its way into the print media in Germany, Japan and Hong Kong, not to mention appearing on the front page of the *Egyptian Gazette*. (Hollands, 2000: 193–4)

Hollands's university had reported the receipt of the award on its web pages. Not knowing this procedure, he was 'caught cold' when phoned by a local newspaper. He described the research to a reporter believing the story had local interest. Unfortunately, Hollands posed for a photograph having a drink in a local bar; the picture was then sold to national and international newspapers 'with racy headlines and bylines'. He says that it was easy to forget that the contents of the glass he was holding 'was actually Perrier with a slice of lemon' (Hollands, 2000: 197).

Another local paper reported the story (without speaking to Hollands) as a 'political story' and the research was described as being 'absurd' and 'common-sense'. The major theme was that the study was a waste of public money, at a time when council services were suffering cutbacks. Even though there was such a 'media frenzy' at the start of the research, the degree of later reporting of the study's findings was 'disappointing'. Fortunately, while the City Council showed an 'initial coolness', the research report was positively received and praised by some council officers and politicians. Hollands was asked to present his report to a council working group (Hollands, 2000: 205, 207).

Media reactions and effects during research

D.H.J. Morgan (1982) 'The British Association scandal: the effect of publicity on a sociological investigation', in R.G. Burgess (ed.), *Field Research: A Sourcebook and Field Manual*. London: Unwin Hyman.

Morgan shows the effect of publicity – how it can disrupt relations during research and be a cause of upset for the researcher. Paradoxically, in his case, it also provided certain benefits due to further insights into the research setting. In late 1964, after finishing participant observation, Morgan presented a paper called 'Women in industry – the factory and the home' to the British Association for the Advancement of Science. He says that he 'discussed in a general way the inter-relationships between a working woman's roles in the workplace and her domestic roles' (Morgan, 1982: 255–6).

The very next day a number of newspapers published various accounts of the presentation. One headline in a national paper ran: 'A factory girl's dream of romance'. Morgan says that what he and a number of others at the factory, from the 'managing director downwards', found 'distressing' was that a couple of newspapers obtained the factory name and printed it. He had not given the name in his talk and had refused to disclose it to reporters. After seeking advice from a senior colleague, they both went to the department immediately. Morgan tried to give the aim of the presentation and outline how the press had distorted his work; he had not sought to criticise the factory workers. He adds:

> I gained more information from and about some of the workers than I had gained during the period prior to the 'scandal'. In many cases this may have reflected a desire on the part of these informants to 'put the record straight'. More specifically, however, these responses may be seen as attempts on the part of the informants to define or redefine their positions in relation to me, the department and the other workers.

Morgan realised the importance, following the newspaper report, of specific divisions in the department that he had not been fully aware of before. Different sections of the factory responded to the publicity in different degrees, according to the patterning of 'age, length of service, residence and type of work' (Morgan, 1982: 256–7).

Even established researchers experience the 'highs' brought by praise and the despondency resulting from negative feedback on a presentation or the rejection of written work such as a submitted research proposal, journal article, or book outline. As Ward admits:

Even after getting feedback on academic writing for over ten years now, I can still feel defensive when I first read it. It is often tempting to say, 'Well, they didn't read this carefully enough,' or 'But they've missed the point completely.' Then I quickly realise that if I had made the point more clearly the feedback would probably not have been given. But it helps to have several commentators, so that you are not at the mercy of a potentially idiosyncratic reader. I ask only those people who appreciate the need for constructive feedback and will give it in the spirit in which it is invited. Some people will always try to score points when giving feedback and they are best avoided (even if they are your friends and family). (Ward, 2002: 95)

For the less experienced researcher negative comments will usually have more effect on self-esteem. Unfortunately, more recent researchers cannot call on an accumulation of previous experiences and successes in terms of completed research or published work to restore self-confidence in their 'management' of emotions.

As a PhD student or other new researcher, detailed feedback is necessary and beneficial for progress and personal development, providing it is given appropriately and with support. The PhD student, for instance, is particularly vulnerable to possible knocks to self-confidence since thesis writing represents a striving to a new high point in intellectual and research development. An area of much concern is feedback given by supervisors to the performance of tasks (e.g. written drafts of chapters). Supervisors will obviously vary to some extent according to their experience and workload, and how they give feedback. Critical feedback can be difficult to cope with, although the researcher may have been aware of at least some of the likely criticism to be made. The researcher should expect some emotional feelings such as anger, embarrassment and disappointment. But, the researcher should not let adverse comments become destructive. Later, the researcher may realise that the criticisms were rather misplaced, or at least not as critical as they first appeared, and relatively straightforward to deal with. Time for reflection is needed to think what can be accepted and what should be argued against and negotiated (see Cryer, 2000: 140–1; Ward, 2002: 94–6). An assessment has to be made as to what are major and what are minor criticisms. Important points may be that there has been a divergence from the main focus or plan, or there is a major omission or error, perhaps regarding methodology or theoretical perspective. Smaller points can be addressed more easily and alterations made without feelings being strongly aroused. Often criticisms may seem rather harsh at first and a writer may believe that his or her work has been misunderstood. It helps to go through the criticisms of your work in detail with someone else whose opinion you value and respect and with whom you work well; this may help you gain some 'perspective' on the feedback.

Reactions and reflections

Robert Moore (1977) 'Becoming a sociologist in Sparkbrook', in C. Bell and H. Newby (eds), *Doing Sociological Research.* **London: George Allen and Unwin.**

Reflections on research experience can take place in the original writing-up of research in a book, article or report, and/or may take place much later in a subsequent commentary. Later reflection can also incorporate the wider reactions to the research on its completion. An interesting and well-known case is the 'reminiscence' by Robert Moore on his 'classic' study of Sparkbrook undertaken with John Rex. Like many other 'community studies', a wide range of methods were used, demonstrating that retrospection can take place not only on ethnographic practice but also on the application of methods more generally. Looking back, it was the personal experience that shone out rather than intricacies of methodology:

> It is difficult to reflect upon this without sounding sentimental or romanticising two years' hard work. I was a new graduate facing the opportunity to 'do' sociology and very unsure how 'it' ought to be done. I discovered that full-time research is not a job; it is a way of life, and so one's life becomes woven into the research just as much as the research becomes part of one's life. For a year I ate, breathed and slept Sparkbrook. I made new friends, made and dissolved relationships, took sides in conflicts, had problems with my landlady and went to parties. In a twelve-year retrospect it is these personal experiences that stand out and the technicalities of research that are most obscured by the passage of ideas. (Moore, 1977: 87)

Moore relates how personal experience and methodology impinge – sometimes dramatically. In his case, when the building in which he was conducting an interview caught fire, he and his interviewee escaped but a third man died. He says that the research was written 'under great pressure' from the sponsors and publishers and was eventually published with some fanfare at the Café Royal at a lunch event attended by 'top people' (Moore, 1977: 101). The book was also serialised in a local newspaper, which led to some local people saying that they were 'very respectable, in spite of what we had said, and that there were many worse areas in Birmingham' (Moore, 1977: 101–2). Television and radio also reported the research and Rex and Moore took part in programmes. Moore concludes that the 'city fathers of Birmingham were clearly very angry. It may therefore have been fortunate that I had moved to Durham to join John Rex by the time the book was published' (Moore, 1977: 103).

Ward makes a number of interesting and useful points for the researcher-author regarding 'negotiating feedback'. He says that whereas for 'the spoken word the first version is often the last' (although pre-recording and editing can take place in television and radio), in contrast, 'the written product can be improved' (Ward, 2002: 94–5). Writing with the benefit of feedback is 'the most powerful way' to improve writing if the feedback process is effective, but he cautions that 'sometimes it can go horribly wrong' (Ward, 2002: 95). Although Ward is concerned with postgraduate research, the questions touched on have implications for feedback to written work in general, for example, whether the researcher-writer would prefer comments on work in writing or face to face. Other questions he raises include how many people to share the draft with, whether to act immediately on feedback or take some time to consider it and how to respond to differences in comments. Finally, there is the interesting question of whether the researcher-writer can give feedback to his or herself (Ward, 2002: 95).

In summary, responses to comments made on written work or oral presentations is a very personal process and feedback can sometimes be hard to take. The points made arouse the researcher's feelings on writing competence and presentation, and thereby, his or her senses of professional identity and inner self.

Feedback on journal article submission

Feedback by referees varies in length and detail, and the researcher may well feel that the article has, at least in part, been misunderstood (even if accepted). But the comments of referees should be taken seriously. They will contain points that have to be addressed, including inconsistencies, repetition, lack of clarity in argument and so on. Even so, referees often differ and their comments should not be taken as simply 'correct' since, in part, some of their 'critical' points may depend rather more on their theoretical or methodological stance. The researcher may have a quandary concerning how much to alter the text since he or she may not fully agree with the points or sometimes completely understand what is being requested. If the article is rejected and the author sends it to another journal and similar comments are made, then there is a greater possibility that there is a serious problem to be addressed.

The editor will send anonymised comments from two or more reviewers and details of his or her subsequent decision. The reviewers may differ in their views: at the extremes, one might say it reads well, another that it is confused, or one that it is original while another that the work contains little that is new. However, there is usually some general agreement on the work and recommendation (if stated). The editor can make a number of decisions:

to publish, perhaps, with some minor revisions; request substantial revision and resubmission; or give a rejection. The proposed article may be said to contain some minor or major deficiencies in writing, style and organisation, or in terms of methods and/or theory. The grounds for rejection may well be simply the overall quality of the article, or that it does not make a sufficient contribution to the field. It may be that it is not suitable for the journal in terms of its subject matter and an editor may suggest a submission to another named journal – maybe the 'stance' or 'style' of the article is not seen as appropriate. Here, the issue of the inclusion of the writer's 'voice' may be a factor. It has been a problem for some researchers in trying to have their work accepted, although the researcher's experience has become a more common feature at least in some journals. For example, Moch queries whether a reviewer of a journal paper she had submitted to a major journal some years previously had 'wished to deny the existence of the researcher experience' since the manuscript was rejected with 'NO OBJECTIVITY' written across (Moch, 2000b: 127).

Types of comments by journal article reviewers

Given the reticence of academics to divulge feedback from journals to colleagues, it is difficult for those submitting articles for the first time to anticipate what a letter from a journal may be like. The author may have to wait several weeks or for months on end for the journal editor to send the decision in the form of a covering letter giving the result and brief reasons for the decision. Frequently, some feedback comments from a number of reviewers (often two) are included, and these may vary from three or four sentences to over a page. The reviewers will see an anonymised article.

Positive feedback – article accepted

Usually this is accompanied by various small suggestions for change, such as some additional material, further references, and small revisions. There may be more substantial revisions asked for to clarify argument or omit sections. Satisfactory revisions are a condition for the acceptance of a resubmitted article.

Silverman (2000) very usefully gives some detailed examples of his own comments on articles he has reviewed for journals.

- Well written
- Interesting topic
- Original approach taken

(Continued)

(Continued)

- Appropriate for the journal
- Draws out the implications for further research and policy
- Should be a useful contribution to the growing literature
- Novel elements
- Good knowledge of the relevant material

Silverman also offers ways to enhance the possibilities of an article being published, for example, reviewer's comments can be taken as 'helpful encouragements' in rewriting (Silverman, 2000: 266–70).

Negative feedback – rejection

In rejecting an article, the editor will commonly say that the decision is supported by the comments and recommendations of anonymous reviewers. Comments may include:

- Poorly written
- Poorly structured
- Not suitable for the journal
- Tries to do too much – too many themes
- The conclusions do not fit the substance of the article
- Does not make the initial aims of the article clear
- The article does not add anything new
- Seems unaware of some of the major writers and issues
- Methodological deficiencies
- Theoretically weak

(see Silverman, 2000: 267–70)

Editors and reviewers can differ considerably in the 'tone' of the comments made to authors. Some appear to forget that there is a person who has feelings involved, someone who has worked hard on the article, even if the outcome is deficient.

Academic refereeing and the experience of rejection

P. Hodkinson (2000) 'Standpoints, power and conflicts in contemporary debates about educational research: an interpretation of repeated rejections', *Auto/Biography,* **VIII (1–2): 3–11.**

(Continued)

Hodkinson faced the repeated rejection of a journal article (on the topic of evaluating qualitative educational research) that was written in collaboration with a young researcher who had recently completed his PhD. He gives one of the few discussions of the process of academic refereeing and the experience of rejection. As he says, the rejection of academic articles is a 'taboo issue' and it is not easy to raise 'without the appearance of special pleading'. For Hodkinson, the 'refereeing process is always much more than a technical process' and can be 'usefully understood' as a 'game', with the 'identities, values, beliefs and feelings', 'positions' and 'differential access to relevant cultural capital' being 'highly significant' (Hodkinson, 2000: 3).

While a very experienced contributor to journals, he admits that, like other recipients, a rejection of an article hurts. He finds it 'irritating' to have to rewrite, particularly if he did not feel the changes were necessary. But, he says that many (but not all) of his previous articles were 'significantly improved' by the editors' and referees' comments. In terms of the current article, the rejections were 'especially difficult to accept'. Previously, he had been successful in placing his few other rejections elsewhere. But on this occasion he appeared to be failing. The rejections, even after some reworking of the article, not only questioned his and his colleague's skills and 'craft', but also went to the heart of their beliefs regarding research practice and 'truth' (Hodkinson, 2000: 6):

> These beliefs are a central part of our academic identities: integral parts of who we are. ... Emotionally, I felt that either I was less adequate a writer and researcher than my self-image required, or I had to cast around for other factors/people to 'blame'. Both these explanations hurt, in different ways. (Hodkinson, 2000: 6)

He concluded that perhaps he and his colleague had been unfortunate, but he asked: 'Am I still incapable of recognising how poor the paper really was? Or is there something more in the continual refusal to give us the chance to rewrite? Perhaps the paper was too controversial and said things that, in the current climate, many leading educational researchers would rather leave unsaid' (Hodkinson, 2000: 6).

Key points to remember on researcher experience: dealing with reactions to research

- Dissemination brings varied forms of reaction – sometimes a rejection of the proposal for a book, an article, or a negative reaction to a presentation. Such reactions are not easy to take, even by those who have numerous publications and have given many presentations.

- It is all right to feel upset for a while when a piece of work has been rejected or a presentation has not gone well, or if feedback from some research activity or draft chapter on a PhD has not been as positive as expected.
- On the other hand, reaction to research dissemination can be very positive, when submitted journal articles are accepted, presentations are well received, and when colleagues are very supportive of the work undertaken.
- Assess the reactions to your research work carefully. For instance, close colleagues are likely to be less critical than those whom you know less well; a journal may be more likely to accept an article if it is on a particular topic that is 'in demand'.
- Do not react straight away to criticism. Leave the comments on an article, or the points made on a presentation, or feedback on other research activities, for a while. Usually the criticisms are not as 'fundamental' as first appears.
- Think as calmly as possible about the reactions made to your work, take advice of others if you feel it would help, and consider what changes you feel would meet the criticisms made.
- Compare your work with similar articles, theses, or presentations. Learn by reading and observing the work of others.
- Seek to improve your writing. Read the comments closely several times, look again at the journal's requirements, and ask for advice from supportive colleagues on your writing.
- Keep in mind that assessments of articles by referees and audiences for presentations are influenced by many factors and not just the content of your work!
- Try not to be discouraged. Do not dwell on 'failures', but assess your writing and presentational skills. Take and act on advice.
- Try again! Write another article, give another presentation!

Summary

Reactions to the dissemination of research can be very varied even to the same piece of work and not always very supportive. Feedback on journal article submissions can be different in terms of detail, length, time taken to arrive and advice given – even two reviewers may differ considerably. Every academic has probably experienced rejection of articles or some bad reviews of work – so you are not alone! It is important to seek advice and make changes and gain skills as required. It may be that the article was submitted to an inappropriate journal or your presentation was to a group who had rather different notions of research practice. After a period of reflection and re-gathering confidence, look again at possible outlets for your work.

An important question to ask – which could be asked at any point in the research process – 'What insights can I make about my strengths and weaknesses and what I have gained by this activity?'

Further reading

V. Jupp et al. (eds) (2000) *Doing Criminological Research* (London: Sage) covers the full range of research processes with articles which put the conduct of research into a wider social and political context. On completing a PhD thesis, the role of supervisors, publishing your findings, and the oral examination and presentations, see P. Oliver (2004) *Writing Your Thesis* (London: Sage) and D. Leonard (2001) *A Woman's Guide to Doctoral Studies* (Buckingham: Open University Press) – the latter has some useful references on getting research published and on media relations. For analysing different kinds of argument, self-criticism and criticism of others, see G.J. Fairbairn and C. Winch (1991) *Reading, Writing and Reasoning: A Guide for Students* (Buckingham: Open University Press), Part 3.

9

WHAT NEXT IN MY RESEARCH?

Chapter overview

End of the 'adventure' – what next?
Academic labour and its organisation
Professional and personal identities in the conduct of research
Rewriting the CV
The researcher's life/life as research career – in academia?
Key points to remember on researcher experience: evaluation of the research
  experience
Summary
Further reading

[the] success in crafting a text has everything to do with a career because, with few exceptions, careers are text-dependent' (Rose, 1990: 14)

The rat race of the university is frequently even more savage than the proverbial one on Madison Avenue, if only because its viciousness is camouflaged by scholarly courtesies and dedication to pedagogic idealism. (Berger, 1966: 194)

End of the 'adventure' – what next?

The journey of research is an 'adventure'. Completion of a study may whet the appetite for further research or a wider consideration of 'what next?'. Even before the current research is anywhere near completion, the researcher or study team may well be engaged in planning further work and submitting another funding proposal. Indeed, their continued salary often depends on a successful bid! Research has its excitements and appeal; it may be that after a successful project, in which an inexperienced investigator has acquired confidence and skills, the next step seems 'naturally' to undertake more research. Some new aspect, not quite central to the current research, may have been identified for further consideration and becomes the focus for another funding application.

In thinking about 'what next?' it is important to reflect back on the research activities and their demands. The practice of investigation can also alter the personal and academic orientation of the researcher, as Robert Moore found in his reflections on his Sparkbrook study:

> My first foray into Sparkbrook underlined the difference between geography and sociology. I knew exactly who I was, but I was lost. I was standing outside the houses when what I wanted to know was probably happening inside. (Moore, 1977: 95)

In addition, it was very important in the formation of his career:

> It certainly did my self-esteem no harm for me to 'pass into the literature' so early in my career, and it remains both flattering and embarrassing when someone at a conference says in a loud voice, 'Oh, you're *the* Robert Moore'. (Moore, 1977: 105)

After the research has been fully completed and the study, thesis, book or report submitted or disseminated, the researcher begins to turn to the next activity and perhaps another significant phase in life. It may well be that the researcher needs some 'break' from research activities, especially after the helter-skelter to meet final deadlines, and has to give attention to other work and non-work commitments. Underneath, the general reflection on research experience is the deeper question for the researcher concerning what he or she 'values' in life and what is central to self and well-being – and how the various personal obligations, aspirations, and social relations can be harmonised.

The PhD student in particular, following the viva and award of the degree, reaches an important biographical turning point. It is a time for consideration of a next step, towards a future academic or research career or in trying something rather different. It could be that the academic route is no longer so appealing or that the research skills could be used in a different context (see Platt, 1976: Chapter 8). The PhD thesis marks a point of transition; the viva can be seen as a ritual through which the student is admitted into full academia:

> Paradoxically, whereas most students look back upon their dissertation experience as gruelling, overwhelming, and oftentimes aversive, students also evaluate the experience as confirming, life-changing, and an important transition into the world of the professional scholar. (Rudestam and Newton, 1992: 144)

For those academics without a PhD but already established in a career, gaining a doctorate is also increasingly seen as a necessary mark of intellectual achievement and confirmation of status.

The aftermath of research completion

Following the successful completion of a major piece of research there is inevitably a sense of relief, perhaps some 'down-feeling' but also moments of 'non-reality' – 'Has it really finished?' The completion of a doctorate or other research can bring a surprising range of emotions. There is a sense of intellectual achievement and relief for actually having had the stamina and perseverance to finish in spite of the various obstacles. Even so, there can be a lingering sense of 'emptiness', since the thesis took up so much of daily life and thoughts. Leonard says, from her experience of supervising postgraduate students, that '[s]ome of the depression is due to a loss of a sense of achieving something each day'. These feelings may be the result of 'a continuing belief in dissertation myths', such as that 'you don't deserve it or that it wasn't really good enough, leading to loss of confidence – despite the fact that to the world you have precisely demonstrated your worth and ability' (Leonard, 2001: 258). Leonard advises taking a holiday and then getting down to publishing the PhD work and moving on to some new research.

The PhD student, in particular, will have to make some adjustment following the pressure to complete the thesis document and achieving a successful viva. The burden of the PhD is no longer there, but oddly may remain at the 'back of the mind' as though there is a task to be done. It will take a while to form a new routine because the long hours of research and writing are no longer present. Even so, before long, thoughts will begin to turn to the next step in terms of career and, possibly, whether to pursue further research or something else entirely.

Following research, the question 'What do I get from my research?' should arise. This can have both positive and negative aspects. We may have become regarded as an expert in a certain field or methodology or, perhaps, we may feel we are becoming possibly too closely identified with these. Like actors, the researcher can be a victim of type casting – as someone who completed that particular study or has that kind of research approach. On the other hand, we may feel reticent about moving on to a new research area or methodology because we may have to build expertise and recognition.

The research we do stays with us in a number of ways in other contexts and over time. For example, Stebbins (1991) found that, following his studies of various amateur and professional pursuits (magicians and football players), the research remained with him in several forms. First, there was an (often short-lived) overlap of his life with those of his former subjects (students) due to being within the university. Secondly, colleagues, friends and relatives assumed that he was still interested in a particular area and willing to talk about it. Finally, media interest was aroused and it was 'awkward' or an 'embarrassment' to admit that he no longer knew what was going on. So Stebbins tried to keep informed of relevant local and national events so he was able to provide information and an opinion: 'By trying to be informed I remain, in a very real sense, in the field.' Thus, while he now has other research interests and he feels the demands on his time from former research activities, nevertheless, it is 'gratifying' to be considered 'still as part of the scene' (Stebbins, 1991: 252–3).

Post-research contacts with participants

Researchers often get to know the participants very well and friendships can develop that outlast the research. Future contact may take place 'accidentally' in an informal setting – passing informants in the street or seeing them out shopping. This is potentially a difficult circumstance ethically since others in the situation may not know of the individual's involvement in the research (which may be on a sensitive topic and therefore involve the principles of confidentiality and anonymity) (see Moch, 2000a). Further, the informant may not wish to be 'recognised', and the researcher – now in another role – may feel embarrassed. Moch (2000a) had the problem of seeing her participants with the experience of breast cancer and also as a group of mid-life women in her activities within her work setting and in the community. She wondered whether she should acknowledge them and also tell them about the progress of the research or ask about their health. It occurred to her that they might be reminded of the illness when they saw her and perhaps feel they should not have related such intimate details. She asked herself whether she had 'exploited' the women and if they 'really feel what I think they feel' (Moch, 2000a: 10).

It can happen that some later contact with the 'researched' can be revealing. For example, 'Punch … reports that he only discovered by chance, at a party long after the fieldwork, how much the police officers he studied had hidden from him' (Hammersley, 1998: 132).

Academic labour and its organisation

The end of a research study is a time to reflect again on our institutional context, our roles and sense of self. As Rose observes on field experiences of the academic researcher:

It is as if we know by our texts and as if fieldwork is an extension of our anthropological, academic everyday life, a deformation of the outer skin of our western culture that never ruptures. In the field we are still academics, safe behind the membrane, we keep the same hours, do the same sorts of things, or do different things temporarily in order to advance our life chances back home. In brief, in the field we work. In the office we work. We work and we write. (Rose, 1990: 16)

Rose reminds us that the academic, like other 'trades', 'labours' and is situated in organisational frameworks:

Ethnographers – like machinists, roofers, executives, and middle managers in corporate life – spend many of their waking hours laboring. The diffuseness of the tasks (such as committee work, talking with students, preparing to teach, faculty meetings, conducting research in the library, interviewing, or writing a paper to be read at the annual meetings) does not lessen its claim on our time or our thought. A number of academics stress that they always think about their work, and that the hours in their office are an indicator of their intellectual labors. We read and write, prepare and lecture inside legally incorporated bodies, institutions, and legal-rational organizations. (Rose, 1990: 18)

Organisations not only shape our activities according to work routines, but also 'socialise' us by attachments to an identity, produce certain orientations on the social world, create certain experience, and expect an institutional biography (through CVs, formal reviews of our 'professional development', job descriptions, and so on). Our working life does not end at the office door. Our thoughts when not at work and, in many respects, our social outlook – our ways of acting and relating – 'spill over' into our private spheres just as our social background and biographical experiences intrude into our working life. We live the life of the sociologist within the research and outside it in daily lives (Berger, 1966: 33).

University as a rat race?

Universities are sometimes seen as an arena of calm – 'ivory towers' of contemplation and study – with common portraits of idiosyncratic scholars pursuing their esoteric interests in dusty libraries, as other-worldly scientists working on the unfathomable pursuit of knowledge, often for its own sake. However, universities are far from (and have never been) immune from the values and practices of the 'outside' world, nor should one expect them to be as 'collegiate' as often assumed or without the baser features of envy, the put-down, back-room deals and discriminatory practices. Cynicism and disappointment, competitiveness and 'power-play' can easily be found. As Berger observed over forty years ago:

(Continued)

When one has tried for a decade to get out of a third-string junior college to one of the prestige universities, or when one has tried in one of the latter to make an associate professorship for the same length of time, the humanistic impulse of sociology will have undergone at least as much strain as it would under the aegis of non-academic employers. One will write those things that have a chance to be published in the right places, one will try to meet those people who dwell close to the mainsprings of academic patronage, one will fill the gaps in one's vita with the same political assiduousness as any junior executive on the make ... (Berger, 1966: 195–6)

Completion of a research project – 'What do I get from research'?

The completion of a research project or thesis should be used as a moment to ask 'What do I get from research?', before considering whether to continue in research activities or to try something else, perhaps a non-research or non-academic path. After the efforts of research, a number of aspects of study may be 're-appreciated':

- research as a quest for knowledge
- research as providing excitement
- research as self-discovery
- research as a commitment to certain methodological practices and theoretical approaches.

Its 'adventurous' appeal once more should come fully to the fore. As Berger says of intellectual work more generally:

Any intellectual activity derives excitement from the moment it becomes a trail of discovery. ... The fascination of sociology lies in the fact that its perspective makes us see in a new light the very world in which we have lived all our lives. This also constitutes a transformation of consciousness. (Berger, 1966: 32–3)

It is a good idea to keep in mind what first motivated you in starting the research, what has been attained (e.g. in technical, emotional or relational skills and competencies), and to have an awareness of what now is possible, in terms of future research.

Professional and personal identities in the conduct of research

Research practice brings a commitment and a sense of identity as a researcher. After a research project, the researcher can reflect 'Do I wish to develop such an identity further?' In doing this, there is an important factor to consider: research is commonly part of a complex and large organisation – the university – with its procedures, hierarchies of power and systems of communication.

The possibilities of a continued research career must be placed in the opportunities provided according to institutional structuring. Research within subject areas and departments at universities is within broader political and socio-cultural frames of funding and evaluation by the university, government agencies and other bodies, which constrain or facilitate opportunities. There is also the need from the researcher to plan ahead and take account of his or her own stage in life and background. Diana Green, one of the few female university vice-chancellors in the UK, advises women who wish to have a successful career in academia that they should know that females (while a majority of graduates) make up only 35 per cent of academic staff in the UK. At the top, only 18 out of around 170 heads of institutions are female. She says that a good route to academic advance for women is to be a research professor. It is important to choose the right subject and adopt the right strategy, but advancement is more likely where there are fewer women to be found (Green, 2004). She acknowledges that there are certain risks. For example, the Research Assessment Exercise in 2001 in the UK, which graded the research publications of researchers, produced wide differences in men and women put forward for assessment (74 per cent to 57 per cent). To be successful she advises that women develop a 'thick skin' and work against devaluing their own talents and lack of self-confidence when seeking promotion, funding and publishing findings. We can add that women often have to work harder and longer than male equivalents to be accepted. Green argues that it is vital to set priorities. Networking is also important as a key part of obtaining advancement and power, but should not be restricted to contacts with other women. In short, she says, it is for the woman to decide what she wants from a career and the kinds of compromises with non-work that are to be made – and after all 'work is not everything' (Green, 2004: 29).

Things to do after a completed research project

The end of research is a time to reflect on what can be done next:

- Consider another project
- Relax
- Take a break

(Continued)

- Catch up with friends
- Pay more attention to family
- Update your CV
- Seek a new job
- Assess job security
- Review career aims
- Assess what has been learnt
- Ask whether you and your social relationships have changed

Rewriting the CV

Rewriting the curriculum vitae is one of the important tasks that should be done following the completion of research to bring achievements up to date and to be ready to apply for a new post. The CV can be considered an 'auto-biographical practice', which has become more extensive and intensive in academia:

> The curriculum vitae has become a central feature of modern academic life. It can be understood as a form of autobiographical practice, one centrally involved with the construction and presentation of a self in a particular occupational context. (Miller and Morgan, 1993: 133)

Like other autobiographical practices, the 'production and evaluation' of the CV 'exists in a particular historical context' (Miller and Morgan, 1993: 134). The notion of 'autobiographical practice' is an interesting one and can be usefully extended to describe the practical experience of the researcher, not merely in describing and analysing research as a 'lived experience', but also a 'reflect on what she [sic] learned in the process' (Reinharz, 1992: 258).

The researcher's life/life as research career – in academia?

Undertaking research in an academic milieu can feel a safe pursuit, even if there is some uncertainty regarding the next research grant, when compared with the 'outside'. For example, the research student may not wish to take up the challenge of considering something new, apart from research, or even moving out of academia and researching for some other body. In fact, there are various 'positive' reasons that can be given for leaving the 'safety' of academic life in the UK. For instance, research does not merely take place within universities but in many institutions (in commercial and professional organisations, local authorities, government bureaucracies, 'think tanks' and independent research centres, charities and campaigning organisations, and trade unions) (see Finnegan, 2005). Ormerod (2004), one 'escapee', now has a successful publishing and consulting career on the 'outside'. He says that most of his reasons for moving from academic life can be summarised under one heading: 'proletarianisation'. Academics have been converted from independent, valued professionals into workers in 'ideas factories'. They are becoming deskilled by a constant process of monitoring, form filling and checking, just as are many other workers. It is certainly apparent that academia in the UK has been drawn into an 'audit culture', with frequent internal and external reviews, increasing evaluation, logging of activities and rising 'through put' of new courses to meet changing 'markets' and to respond to increasing student numbers. For Ormerod, the wider world outside academia may seem rather off-putting for academics. They are used to institutional life, having spent most of their lives in educational organisations. However, he says, their skills can be used in business, where the skills of communication and persuasion are also required. Since academics already 'sell' their wares at conferences and search out research funds, they have some basis for an 'another' life. In fact, Ormerod argues, the new outside context can be liberating; instead of relying on research councils and several major funding organisations, now there is a great range of potential funders, and a wider audience for the work undertaken. He encourages academics to take the jump into this new arena for their research and ideas – a successful research career is possible outside academia, and often with a greater sense of personal control (Ormerod, 2004).

On completion of a research project the researcher has the opportunity to consider wider opportunities to work in commercial, charitable or other institutions, but may prefer to remain in the academic context of the university setting. In fact, there are now more opportunities to collaborate with outside bodies on research without leaving academia.

Key points to remember on researcher experience: evaluation of the research experience

Finishing a research project should allow for a period of evaluation of the 'research experience':

- A review of how stresses and strains were coped with, and the excitement and sense of achievement gained.

- Academic research is often not particularly financially rewarding. Are there other research opportunities?
- What were the motivations to do the research? Have those motivations changed in type and degree?
- The PhD is increasingly required as a starting point for an academic career.
- Academic and research careers are part of a competitive and institutional context.
- Finally, ask yourself: 'Do I enjoy research?' 'Do I see research as an important activity to be engaged in?'

Summary

The completion of a research project or thesis should be a time for reflection on your motivations for research, self-identity, and career. Perhaps, most of all, a period of thought on the general experience of research is required: whether, despite the travails, there was sufficient excitement and satisfaction to make it an experience that should be repeated. It is also a point when a decision to do something else should at least be contemplated. However, much will depend on the opportunities that are available, and on financial and other commitments in deciding the 'next step'.

There are numerous preconceptions of research – research as difficult, complicated, laborious, fun, exciting, unnecessary, finding what you want to, objective, scientific, strictly organised, a waste, fascinating, exploitative, costly, or specialised. Such preconceptions may deter or motivate the prospective researcher. Having completed the research, the researcher may find some of these notions have been supported. Some aspects of research may come as a surprise – perhaps both the extent of hard, routine work and the degree of exhilaration that can result from new insights, new skills, self-confidence and achievement.

In looking back on the research, the sheer commitment needed and the inevitable daily problems are usually placed in a different perspective, as the feelings of 'survival' are replaced by a sense of accomplishment. Even if the research was not fully successful, usually there are 'positives' that have been gained from the personal, technical and relational skills attained. These can be transferred to another activity, whether it is research or something else. In this way, we become more aware of the opportunities, alternatives, satisfactions and difficulties of research and how to be conscious of and 'control' our personal involvement. As Kleinman says, even the reconsideration of the less attractive parts of our research can have benefits:

Does it seem burdensome that, in addition to spending time and effort in the field, field researchers also must deal with their fears and other unpleasant feelings? Because we are the instruments of research, it can be no other way. And this unfair burden may have a brighter side, for it allows us to gain deeper knowledge about others and ourselves. (Kleinman, 1991: 194)

Further reading

D. Leonard (2001) *A Woman's Guide to Doctoral Studies* (Buckingham: Open University Press) has a useful section on 'Returning to your previous life' and future careers; D. Silverman (2000) *Doing Qualitative Research: A Practical Handbook* (London: Sage) has a short chapter with hints on 'Finding a job'. A comprehensive introduction to an academic career is L. Blaxter et al. (eds) (1998) *The Academic Career Handbook* (Buckingham: Open University Press).

10

CONCLUSION: THE RESEARCHER'S EXPERIENCE OF RESEARCH

Chapter overview

Researcher experience in research
Researcher experience and the emotions
Researcher insights and reflections
Orientations to the researched revisited
Conclusion: the researcher's experience of research
Key points to remember on researcher experience: ten things for the researcher to remember
Summary

Reports about field research usually describe the methods and techniques of the research. Less often do they tell of the researchers' social and emotional experiences: anxiety and frustration, as well as exhilaration and pride in achievement. These topics are discussed more often in personal conversations between field researchers than written about in the literature. (Shaffir and Stebbins, 1991: xi)

It will be difficult for many sociologists to accept that we presently know little or nothing about ourselves or other sociologists or, in point of fact, that we know little about how one piece of social research, or one sociologist, comes to be esteemed while another is disparaged or ignored. (Gouldner, in Seale, 2004: 382)

Researcher experience in research

A consideration of 'the researcher's experience of research' has typically been found within qualitative research, placing importance on the 'subjective' aspects of the researcher's role. This examination has pointed to the personal and interactive elements in the conduct of research and how the researcher's identity and biography both influence and are shaped by the investigation. However, it has been argued that many of the observations on research experience made in qualitative research can be extended to quantitative, documentary and other approaches, where such a consideration has been neglected. Of course, researchers often use a 'mix' of methods of data collection in a specific project. Despite the 'imperatives' of value neutrality and objectivity, the quantitative researcher is also a 'biographical subject' affected by the experience of research. To give the 'reality' of the acting, deciding, feeling, relational being – the investigator – should not imply that all methodological procedure is according to 'subjective' whim. Neither should the presentation of research experience be seen merely as an opportunity to admit methodological shortcomings. We do not need to know everything about the researcher, or see researchers merely looking for what suits their emotional needs or, as admitting personal deficiencies. But, as Reinharz says, referring to feminist research:

Writing such as this is not a confession of 'bias' as it would undoubtedly be labeled in a positivist framework. Rather it is an explanation of 'the researcher's standpoint' in a feminist framework. (Reinharz, 1992: 259)

The exploration of the experience of research as a starting point disrupts the traditional conception of the 'idealised' researcher gathering the facts from the social world to bring back to the institution for later investigation.

The question of the representation of research experience leads to the issue of how the 'voice' of the researcher is to be given in a report. Reinharz says, 'reflections' may be read as 'partly informal, engagingly personal, and even confessional' (Reinharz, 1992: 258–9). Even so, the representation of 'researcher voice' must be a 'critical' one since there are deeper questions if research, while beginning with researcher experience remains constrained by a non-reflexivity. Researcher experience can be problematic because 'it can lay the groundwork for solipsism or projection … [and] easily verge on ethnocentrism' (Reinharz, 1992: 261). Thus, to start unreflexively from personal experience and not strive to go beyond it can serve as an important restriction in what can be discovered about other lives and relevant social issues.

Researcher experience and the emotions

The focus on research roles and experience brings to the fore the place of the 'feelings' or emotions in social life. As a social actor, the researcher is also an emotional, relational being, responding to and creating the surrounding world. 'Emotion' is part of all research, from the work of the most 'interpretative' researcher on the one hand, to the procedures of the most determined investigator working within the positivist, quantitative approach where 'evaluative knowledge is assumed to be objectively valid', on the other (Denzin, 2001: 51). However committed to being 'free' from the 'real' world of interaction and emotions, the researcher can never be hermetically sealed from situational meaning construction and his and her own feelings.

The 'lessons' of emotional experience in research

Denzin insightfully provides a number of 'lessons' on emotion in research:

1 The 'observer cannot write meaningful interpretation until he or she has emotionally entered into and been part of the experiences he or she writes about'.
2 Readers 'cannot be expected to identify with and understand a set of written interpretations emotionally unless those interpretations are written in a way that elicits emotional identification and understanding. A reader cannot be expected to feel or understand something that the writer does not feel.'
3 The researcher or 'writer can produce nonspurious emotional understandings only if he or she brings alive the world of lived experience in the pages of the text'.
4 A 'writer cannot create emotional understandings if readers are not willing to enter into the writer's text and the world of lived experience he or she depicts'. (Denzin, 2001: 141–2)

Thus, research takes place in an 'intersubjective world' of meaning construction, in which expectations and understandings include the communication of feelings or emotion.

A major part of the emotional experience of research is one of 'labouring', whether it is in observing a setting, writing up fieldnotes, sorting out all kinds of paper, files and materials, in-putting computer data for statistical or qualitative analysis, or writing, editing and correcting research manuscripts. Academic and research life (although often more comfortable, less physically demanding and better paid than many occupations), like all 'work', contains physical and emotional labour. Academics complain that it is often difficult to turn off when they are 'out of hours', while also pointing to their research labour time as some kind of vindication for their role, expertise and social standing. It is as though the more hours 'in the field' or in the office demonstrates both commitment and support for their intellectual output (Rose, 1990: 18). The labour of research and other academic work draws attention to the fact that, after all, as intellectuals and researchers we are workers within and on behalf of organisations. For Van Maanen et al.:

> Critics argue that conventional social research dulls the imagination; locks the observed inside rigid category systems having little or nothing to do with the culture of the researched, but everything to do with our research culture; promotes an insidious institutionalization of social boundaries that separate 'us' (the observers) from 'them' (the observed); and perhaps most telling has become tedious, if not boring, thus losing its power to convince. (Van Maanen et al., 1990: 5)

We do not need to agree fully with Van Maanen et al.'s view regarding the effects of 'conventional social research', but we can readily accept that 'imagination' is central to the work of the researcher and how he or she sees the social world.

Researcher insights and reflections

The experience of research is extremely varied, with differing emotions, shifting situations, multiple relationships (within and external to the actual research) and the performance of a whole range of tasks during the 'life' of the study. Also, the connection with those involved may last for a significant period afterwards, if only through some remembrance of the experience. A first research project or postgraduate study can be significant in terms of the formation of important, long-lasting academic and personal relationships.

Roles in the research process can be described in various ways and shift according to the tasks being performed. Commentators have pointed to a number of conceptions of the researcher: for instance, as a 'theorist' who analyses and employs abstract thought; or as an 'objective expert', a 'scientist' who tries to avoid influencing the research and applies a 'formula'; or as a 'precise, methodical, logical, highly trained' individual who is in 'control of the research process' (O'Leary, 2004: 92). The researcher can also be a 'change agent', perhaps working in a 'participatory' or 'collaborative' manner to improve a situation. Researchers may exhibit several aspects of these different roles during the course of a study. O'Leary adds two interesting further ideas: the researcher as a 'bricoleur' who, according to situation, 'will employ a variety of methodological tools and even create new ones as needed to solve a puzzle or find a solution', and as a 'choreographer' or 'the coordinator of the dance' – someone who has a wider vision and tries to explore something new (O'Leary, 2004: 92). While recognising the need for 'practicality' (precision, rigour and some form of training), it is the outward, creative, 'adventurous' orientations – the researcher as 'bricoleur' and 'choreographer' – that I find particularly appealing.

The four necessities of research

In advising postgraduate students, who spend a long time on their study, Cryer (2000) says that they must construct a mode of living that is appropriate to their work. She describes 'three necessities of research' in relation to post-graduate students' work that can be applied more generally to all research:

1 Health and stamina.
2 Motivation to succeed.
3 Personal and financial support from non-research contexts. (Cryer, 2000: 37)

I would like to add another: 'enjoyment'. Enjoyment is a necessity for the researcher. Without it, interest can wane, the research can become a seemingly never-ending chore, the likely success of the research may be comprised and the researcher can be deterred from further research work. Enjoyment is closely associated with the stimulation that research into an area can bring, for instance, the questioning stance and a concern to find something new. It can bring confidence and a sense of fulfilment, and an encouragement to undertake research again. Enjoyment enhances a sense of self-worth and self-understanding.

A focus on the importance of 'research experience', it has been argued in this book, should be closely linked with a 'reflexivity'. While this term has been widely used in different ways, here it has been seen as 'self-monitoring' – a reflection on personal life and its interrelation between research and non-work contexts and a means of considering the use of methods, the 'gathering' of data, the process of interpretation, writing-up and dissemination.

Researcher identity and 'stories' of organisational research

The researcher is part of a major institution – the university – and can be considered an 'expert' on organisational life, certainly if a 'reflective' and 'insightful' approach is taken to work within his or her organisational setting and its part in self and professional identity formation. Such an understanding of his or her own organisation can enable the researcher to compare and contrast processes in his or her own setting with those found elsewhere in research.

(Continued)

(Continued)

Elsbach (2000) relates six 'stories' by qualitative researchers who had engaged in organisational studies and found several general insights regarding their work and research setting relating to personal and professional identities. These included insights into 'one's relationship with informants', 'personal and professional growth' and, perhaps, into 'affirming one's self-perception as unconventional' (Elsbach, 2000: 71). Elsbach found that a number of researchers reported identities that they had not expected at the start of their careers:

> Some researchers felt a responsibility to act as a therapist or counselor, whereas others felt they should at least be empathetic and act as ambassadors in relating informants' stories to the public. A couple mentioned the importance of suppressing personal opinions and beliefs that conflicted with those of their informants to make those informants feel more comfortable. (Elsbach, 2000: 71)

Even so, 'most of them admitted enjoying the new relationships with informants and found them an important motivator for continuing qualitative research', and 'claimed to have a greater appreciation for the workers they observed'. A couple said that 'working at these relationships helped their communication skills and relationships outside of their professional roles' (Elsbach, 2000: 71).

Elsbach argues that the closeness of the interaction with informants, for instance, relaying 'negative results', made qualitative researchers 'better listeners and conversationalists' and some reported that they had 'matured as scholars and people'. A further finding related to the confidence that research gave in 'accepting' an identity as a qualitative researcher, while many colleagues may not have valued such a designation. Most claimed that participating in qualitative research allowed them to 'affirm their identities as unconventional people', as 'outsiders', and to differentiate themselves from the stereotype of the 'business school professor'. Elsbach concludes that the 'experiences of qualitative or organizational researchers may lead those researchers to see themselves as more adept communicators, mature scholars, and unconventional individuals in comparison to their quantitative researchers' (Elsbach, 2000: 72–3).

However, it can be argued that both qualitative and other researchers can and should consider their own position and its formation, including how they 'present' themselves to others and how academic and institutional practices shape self-definition and researcher identity. We can say that qualitative and quantitative researchers – as members of institutional settings – by critically reflecting on the formation of their own identities (and self-perceptions), can gain insights into how the identities of others inside and outside the university are formed.

The exploration of the experience of research through a reflexive approach to ongoing action (including decisions, choices, orientation and feelings) raises questions concerning our identity. Whereas the discussion of 'research identity' has mainly taken place in the context of qualitative research, quantitative and other research (visual, documentary, unobtrusive) practice also has implications for the researcher in terms of identity and in developing research practices. The researcher as self and socially defined (according to age, gender, sexuality and other social dimensions), the performance of research 'roles', the complex interrelations with others in and outside research settings, the awareness of biographical changes, and the shaping influences of the surrounding institutional context, are relevant to researcher identity within all research.

Orientations to the researched revisited

An important element of researcher experience relates to the responsibilities to the 'researched'. As Middleton, writing as an anthropologist, states:

> Not every anthropologist will be fortunate enough to move from shyness and strangeness to respect and love, but the genuine concern for the people among whom we work and a willingness to treat them as individuals and not as subjects should be possible. (Middleton, 1978: 238)

While many informants 'neither want nor need to continue a relationship with us and at best tolerate us while we are conducting our research', we may also bear a continuing responsibility to those with whom we have formed a close personal relationship (Taylor, 1991: 246). Ties with those studied and views or feelings towards them can vary during the course of research and later. In addition, the investigator may have a number of expectations of those being studied: perhaps an idealisation of those who are suffering; or maybe negative feelings towards them due to their activities; or merely that they share the same view of the world. The upsetting of expectations can bring feelings of disappointment, resentment, frustration, a sense of relief, or greater empathy for the people studied. It can also lead to a greater self-knowledge and understanding of the researched, their views and situation.

Conclusion: the researcher's experience of research

The examination of the experience of research, in its many varied guises, leads to the conclusion that what 'actually happens' may bear little resemblance to the laid-down schemas, definitions, processes and timetables provided by textbooks and published reports. Some forty years ago Howard Becker (see Denzin, 1970), reviewing Hammond's pioneering edited volume *Sociologists at Work* (1964), declared:

As every researcher knows, there is more to doing research than is dreamt of in philosophies of science, and texts in methodology offer answers to only a fraction of the problems one encounters. The best laid research plans run up against unforeseen contingencies in the collection and analysis of data; the data one collects may prove to have little to do with the hypothesis one sets out to test; unexpected findings inspire new ideas. No matter how carefully one plans in advance, research is designed in the course of its execution. The finished monograph is the result of hundreds of decisions, large and small, made while the research is under way and our standard texts do not give us procedures and techniques for making these decisions. ... that social research being what it is, we can never escape the necessity to improvise, the surprise of the unexpected, our dependence on inspiration. ... It is possible, after all, to reflect on one's difficulties and inspirations and see how they could be handled more rationally the next time around. In short, one can be methodical about matters that earlier had been left to chance and improvisation and thus cut down the area of guesswork. (Denzin, 1970: 314)

Despite the subsequent greater recognition of the intricacies of the researcher's experience in discussions of research methodology, the increasing acceptance of qualitative approaches, and growing critiques of positivist methods, Becker's view remains important. It can serve as a reminder of the need for a combination of imagination and organisation in the research process. A prime motivation for research, I have argued, is the excitement of adventure and discovery – with new sets of relationships, new insights to be gained, and difficulties to be overcome.

Key points to remember on researcher experience: ten things for the researcher to remember

These are some of the things to bear in mind when undertaking research to enable you to see beyond any current problem:

1. This is what you chose to do – 'let's get it done'!
2. Research is hard work but it should also be pleasurable.
3. Learn from your previous successes – believe in your abilities!
4. Current difficulties often do not seem as great several days later.
5. Seek out other researchers – socialise.
6. The more you write the easier it should become.
7. Do not be afraid to seek advice, help and support.

8. Following writing guidelines is essential but try something a little different.
9. Organise your time to balance research and outside commitments.
10. You will find out a great deal about yourself!

Above all, keep in mind that research is not merely a journey, it is an adventure!

Summary

Research can seem full of difficulties – so much so that some academics are put off it altogether and prefer to teach or 'theorise', or perhaps seek to reduce some research problems by only using secondary sources. However, all research, whether using qualitative, quantitative or 'mixed' methods, can have large rewards and satisfactions. Research tips can be gained from more established researchers, courses and textbooks (such as this one), but they can only partly prepare for the practice and experience of research.

The experience of research has both its 'good' and 'bad' moments, and not everyone wishes to be a full-time or even part-time researcher for long. Nevertheless, 'research' in its myriad forms is very much part of many professional careers, both in the acquisition of qualifications and more routinely as part of 'projects', 'presentations' and 'keeping up to date'. While not everyone is suited to doing research, it does bring personal rewards in terms of excitement in finding out new things, delving deeper into a subject of interest and in presenting findings to share with others – it is a process of discovery, an adventure.

The research adventure and 'fun'

Research as an adventure should be demanding yet enjoyable, and sociologists should be serious about their work but be able to see themselves and their activities at times in a more lighthearted way: 'Research is hard work, it's always a bit suffering. Therefore, on the other side, research should be fun' (Strauss, in Strauss et al., 2004).

GLOSSARY

Dissemination   Dissemination is the communication of findings gained from research to appropriate audiences.

Emotions   There is much current discussion (psychological, sociological) on the basis and expression of the 'emotions'. Here, there has been a pragmatic focus on the feelings or moods of the researcher during planning, operation, writing and receiving reaction to research rather than the deeper theoretical issues. The influences on the researcher's emotions, and how he or she can deal with them, has been given priority, instead of a more detailed examination of their psychological or socio-cultural formation.

Fieldnotes   These are records usually based on 'fieldwork' but can be applied to any process of data collection. They are commonly described as 'mental notes', 'jotted notes' (prepared in the field) or 'full fieldnotes' (giving details of observations) (Becker and Bryman, 2004: 394).

Fieldwork research   Fieldwork is usually identified with forms of participant observation; often such terms are used interchangeably to refer to research in everyday social settings (schools and work situations, or in communities). But, in fact, fieldwork may cover a much greater range of data collection (e.g. more formal interviews), and the collection of a wider set of materials (e.g. statistics, official and other records and personal materials, such as diaries and photographs). As Burgess says: 'Field research involves the activities of the researcher, the influence of the researcher on the researched, the practices and procedures of doing research and the methods of data collection and data analysis' (Burgess, 1982: 2).

Positivism   'Positivism' refers to research practice that relies on the principles of the 'scientific method'. It depends upon observation and measurement to study social phenomena and a view of the researcher as detached, value-neutral and objective.

Reflexive account A reflexive account is the information given (as a commentary, a footnote, or a separate autobiographical statement) to an audience of the researcher's experience in the research. Such 'reflexive' accounts provide the reader or listener with insights into how the researcher's life and experience interrelated with the research practice and decisions, and the conduct of research (see Oliver, 2004: 159).

Reflexivity This term has been subject to a great deal of debate in sociology. Here it has been taken to refer to 'self-monitoring' – the 'reflection' on the activities of the researcher, including the interconnections between research practice and external involvements, as well as the consideration of actions within research processes (e.g. the formation of data). It may be argued that in 'the absence of reflexivity, the strengths of the data are exaggerated and/or the weaknesses underemphasised' (Becker and Bryman, 2004: 404).

Researcher's biography The 'researcher's biography' can be used to denote the researcher's past life and present involvement in research and other relations, which may affect the conduct and outcome of the research process.

Viva This is a form of interview in which doctoral students are orally examined by internal and external examiners who have read the thesis and ask questions to satisfy themselves that the student has reached the necessary standard.

BIBLIOGRAPHY

Atkinson, P. (1990) *The Ethnographic Imagination*. London: Sage.

Back, L. (2002) 'Dancing and wrestling with scholarship: things to do and things to avoid in a PhD Career', *Sociological Research Online*, 7 (4). http://www.socres-online.org.uk/7/4back.html

Becker, H.S. (1967) 'Whose side are we on?', *Social Problems*, 14 (Winter): 239–48.

Becker, H.S. (1986) *Writing for Social Scientists: How To Start and Finish Your Thesis, Book, or Article*. Chicago: University of Chicago Press.

Becker, H.S. (1998) *Tricks of the Trade: How To Think about Your Research While You're Doing It*. Chicago: The University of Chicago Press.

Becker, S. and Bryman, A. (eds) (2004) *Understanding Research for Social Policy and Practice*. Bristol: The Policy Press.

Bell, C. (1977) 'Reflections on the Banbury restudy', in C. Bell and H. Newby (eds), *Doing Sociological Research*. London: George Allen and Unwin.

Bell, C. and Encel, S. (eds) (1978) *Inside the Whale: Ten Personal Accounts of Social Research*. Oxford: Pergamon Press.

Bell, J. (1999) *Doing Your Research Project* (3rd edn). Buckingham: Open University Press.

Bendix, R. and Roth, G. (1971) *Scholarship and Partisanship: Essays on Max Weber*. Berkeley: University of California Press.

Benton, T. and Craib, I. (2001) *Philosophy of Social Science*. Basingstoke: Palgrave.

Berger, P.L. (1966) *Invitation to Sociology*. Harmondsworth: Penguin.

Beverley, J. (2000) 'Testimonio, subalternity, and narrative authority', in N.K. Denzin and Y.S. Lincoln (eds), *Handbook of Qualitative Research* (2nd edn). London: Sage.

Birley, G. and Moreland, N. (1998) *A Practical Guide to Academic Research*. London: Kogan Page.

Blaxter, L., Hughes, C. and Tight, M. (1998) *The Academic Career Handbook*. Buckingham: Open University Press.

Blaxter, L., Hughes, C. and Tight, M. (2001) *How to Research* (2nd edn). Buckingham: Open University Press.

Bloor, M. (2004) 'Addressing social problems through qualitative research', in D. Silverman (ed.), *Qualitative Research: Theory, Method and Practice* (2nd edn). London: Sage.

Bottomley, B. (1978) 'Words, deeds and postgraduate research', in C. Bell and S. Encel (eds), *Inside the Whale: Ten Personal Accounts of Social Research*. Oxford: Pergamon Press.

Brewer, J.D. (2000) *Ethnography*. Buckingham: Open University Press.

Brown, S., Black, D., Day, A. and Race, P. (1998) *500 Tips for Getting Published: A Guide for Educators, Researchers and Professionals*. London: Kogan Page.

Bruyn, S.T. (1966) *The Human Perspective in Sociology*. Englewood Cliffs, NJ: Prentice-Hall.

Bryman, A. (1988) *Quantity and Quality in Social Research*. London: Unwin Hyman.

Bryman, A. (2004) *Social Research Methods* (2nd edn). Oxford: Oxford University Press.

Bryman, A. (ed.) (2006) *Mixed Methods* (4 vols). London: Sage.

Bryman, A. and Burgess, R.G. (eds) (1994) *Analyzing Qualitative Data*. London: Routledge.

Bryman, A. and Burgess, R.G. (eds) (1999) *Qualitative Research* (4 vols). London: Sage.

Burgess, R.G. (ed.) (1982) *Field Research: a Sourcebook and Field Manual*. London: Unwin Hyman.

Burton, D. (ed.) (2000) *Research Training for Social Scientists: A Handbook for Postgraduate Researchers*. London: Sage.

Church, K. (1995) *Forbidden Narratives: Critical Autobiography as Social Science*. London: Gordon and Breach.

Coffey, A. (1999) *The Ethnographic Self*. London: Sage.

Cohen, A.P. (1992) 'Self-conscious anthropology', in J. Okely and H. Callaway (eds), *Anthropology and Autobiography*. London: Routledge.

Cohen, S. and Taylor, L. (1972) *Psychological Survival*. Harmondsworth: Penguin.

Cohen, S. and Taylor, L. (1978) *Escape Attempts: The Theory and Practice of Resistance to Everyday Life*. Harmondsworth: Penguin.

Coley, S.M. and Scheinberg, C.A. (2000) *Proposal Writing*. London: Sage.

Cottrell, S. (2003) *Skills for Success*. Basingstoke: Palgrave Macmillan.

Crabtree, B.F. and Miller, W.L. (eds) (1999) *Doing Qualitative Research* (2nd edn). London: Sage.

Crème, P. and Lea, M.R. (1997) *Writing at University*. Buckingham: Open University Press.

Cryer, P. (2000) *The Research Student's Guide to Success*. Buckingham: Open University Press.

Czarniawska, B. (2004) 'Writing a social science monograph', in C. Seale et al. (eds), *Qualitative Research Practice*. London: Sage.

Davies, P. (2000) 'Doing interviews with female offenders', in V. Jupp, P. Davies and P. Francis (eds), *Doing Criminological Research*. London: Sage.

Day, A. (1996) *How To Get Research Published in Journals*. Farnborough: Gower.

Day, E. (2002) 'Me, My*self and I: personal and professional re-constructions in ethnographic research', in *Forum: Qualitative Research*, 3 (3), http://www.qualitative-research.net/fqs-texte/3-02/3-02day-e.htm.

Denscombe, M. (2003) *The Good Research Guide* (2nd edn). Buckingham: Open University Press.

Denzin, N.K. (1970) *The Research Act in Sociology*. London: Butterworths.

Denzin, N.K. (2001) *Interpretive Interactionism* (2nd edn). London: Sage.

Denzin, N.K. and Lincoln, Y.S. (eds) (2000a) *Handbook of Qualitative Research* (2nd edn). London: Sage.

Denzin, N.K. and Lincoln, Y.S. (2000b) 'The Seventh Moment: Out of the Past', in N.K. Denzin and Y.S. Lincoln (eds), *Handbook of Qualitative Research* (2nd edn). London: Sage.

Denzin, N.K. (2003) *Performance Ethnography: Critical Pedagogy and the Politics of Culture*. London: Sage.

Dunleavy, P. (2003) *Authoring a PhD: How to Plan, Draft, Write and Finish a Doctoral Thesis or Dissertation*. Basingstoke: Palgrave Macmillan.

Easterday, L., Papademas, D., Schorr, L. and Valentine, C. (1982) 'The making of a female researcher: role problems in fieldwork', in R.G. Burgess (ed.), *Field Research: A Sourcebook and Field Manual*. London: Unwin Hyman.

Economic and Social Research Council (ESRC) (1993) *Pressing Home Your Findings: Media Guidelines for ESRC Researchers*. Swindon: Economic and Social Research Council.

Elliott, J. (2005) *Using Narrative in Social Research: Qualitative and Quantitative Approaches*. London: Sage.

Ellis, C. and Bochner, A.P. (2000) 'Autoethnography, personal narrative, reflexivity', in N.K. Denzin and Y.S. Lincoln (eds), *The Handbook of Qualitative Research* (2nd edn). London: Sage.

Elsbach, K.D. (2000) 'Six stories of researcher experience in organizational studies: personal and professional insights', in S.D. Moch and M.F. Gates (eds), *The Researcher Experience in Qualitative Research*. London: Sage.

Etherington, L. (2004) *Becoming a Reflexive Researcher: Using Our Selves in Research*. London: Jessica Kingsley Publishers.

Fairbairn, G.J. and Winch, C. (1991) *Reading, Writing and Reasoning: A Guide for Students*. Buckingham: Open University Press.

Fielding, N. (2004) 'Working in hostile environments', in C. Seale et al. (eds), *Qualitative Research Practice*. London: Sage.

Fink, A. (2005) *Conducting Research Literature Reviews* (2nd edn). London: Sage.

Finnegan, R. (ed.) (2005) *Participating in the Knowledge Society: Researchers Beyond the University Walls*. Basingstoke: Palgrave Macmillan.

Foskett, N. and Foskett, R. (2006) *Postgraduate Study in the UK: The International Student's Guide*. London: Sage.

Freedman, J. (2001) *Feminism*. Buckingham: Open University Press.

Giddens, A. (1987) *Social Theory and Modern Sociology*. Cambridge: Polity Press.

Gilbert, N. (ed.) (2006) *The Postgraduate Guidebook*. London: Sage.

Goffman, E. (1971) *The Presentation of Self in Everyday Life*. Harmondsworth: Penguin.

Green, D. (2004) 'Smashing ceilings: how women can get ahead', in *How To Get Promoted: A Career Guide for Academics* (Booklet). *The Times Higher Education Supplement*, 19 November.

Hallowell, N., Lawton, J. and Gregory, S. (eds) (2005) *Reflections on Research: The Realities of Doing Research in the Social Sciences*. Maidenhead: Open University Press.

Hammersley, M. (1998) *Reading Ethnographic Research* (2nd edn). London: Longman.

Hammond, P.E. (ed.) (1964) *Sociologists at Work: Essays on the Craft of Social Research*. London: Basic Books.

Hart, C. (1998) *Doing a Literature Review*. London: Sage.

Hart, C. (2001) *Doing a Literature Search*. London: Sage.

Harvey, L. (1990) *Critical Social Research*. London: Unwin Hyman.

Hatch, J.A. and Wisniewski, R. (1995) 'Life history and narrative: questions, issues, and exemplary works', in J.A. Hatch and R. Wisniewski (eds), *Life History and Narrative*. London: The Falmer Press.

Hawkins, B. and Sorgi, M. (1985) *Research: How To Plan, Speak and Write about It*. Berlin/New York: Springer Verlag.

Hey, V. (2002) '"Not as nice as she was supposed to be": schoolgirls' friendships', in S. Taylor (ed.), *Ethnographic Research: A Reader*. London: Sage.

Hochschild, A. (1983) *The Managed Heart*. Berkeley: University of California Press.

Hodkinson, P. (2000) 'Standpoints, power and conflicts in contemporary debates about educational research: an interpretation of repeated rejections', *Auto/Biography*, VIII (1–2): 3–11.

Hollands, R.G. (2000) '"Lager louts, tarts, and hooligans": the criminalization of young adults in a study of Newcastle night-life', in V. Jupp, P. Davies and P. Francis (eds), *Doing Criminological Research*. London: Sage.

Holliday, A. (2001) *Doing and Writing Qualitative Research*. London: Sage.

Horowitz, I.L. (ed.) (1970) *Sociological Self Images: A Collective Portrait*. Oxford: Pergamon Press.

Hughes, G. (2000) 'Understanding the politics of criminological research', in V. Jupp, P. Davies and P. Francis (eds), *Doing Criminological Research*. London: Sage.

Ivanič, R. (1997) *Writing and Identity: The Discoursal Construction of Identity in Academic Writing*. Amsterdam: John Benjamins.

Jupp, V., Davies, P. and Francis, P. (eds) (2000) *Doing Criminological Research*. London: Sage.

Kaplan, D. (ed.) (2004) *The Sage Handbook of Quantitative Methodology for the Social Sciences*. London: Sage.

Kenna, M.E. (1992) 'Changing places and altered perspectives: research on a Greek island in the 1960s and in the 1980s', in J. Okely and H. Callaway (eds), *Anthropology and Autobiography*. London: Routledge.

Kinman, G. and Jones, F. (2004) 'Working to the limit', Association of University Teachers (AUT) http://www.aut.org.uk/media/html/r/t/workingtothelimit_summary.html

Kleinman, S. (1991) 'Field-workers' feelings: what we feel, who we are, how we analyze', in W.B. Shaffir and R.A. Stebbins (eds), *Experiencing Fieldwork: An Inside View of Qualitative Research*. London: Sage.

Kleinman, S. and Copp, M.A. (1993) *Emotions and Fieldwork*. London: Sage.

Layder, D. (2004) *Emotion in Social Life: The Lost Heart of Society*. London: Sage.

Lea, M.R. and Stierer, B. (eds) (2000) *Student Writing in Higher Education*. Buckingham: Society for Research in Higher Education (SRHE) and Open University Press.

Lee, R.M. (2000) *Unobtrusive Methods on Social Research*. Buckingham: Open University Press.

Leonard, D. (2001) *A Woman's Guide to Doctoral Studies*. Buckingham: Open University Press.

Locke, L.F., Spirduso, W.W. and Silverman, S.J. (1993) *Proposals that Work* (3rd edn). London: Sage.

Lyman, S. and Scott, M. (1984) 'Adventures', in J. Douglas (ed.), *Sociology of Deviance*. Boston: Allyn and Bacon.

Markham, A. (2004) 'The internet as a research context', in C. Seale, G. Gobo, J.F. Gubrium and D. Silverman (eds), *Qualitative Research Practice*. London: Sage.

Martin, C. (2000) 'Doing research in a prison setting', in V. Jupp, P. Davies and P. Francis (eds), *Doing Criminological Research*. London: Sage.

May, T. (2001) *Social Research* (3rd edn). Buckingham: Open University Press.

McCall, B. (2006) 'Academics suffer more stress than A & E staff', *The Times Higher Education Supplement,* 17 February: 64.

McCarthy, P. and Hatcher, C. (2002) *Presentation Skills: The Essential Guide for Students*. London: Sage.

Merton, R. (1988) 'Some thoughts on the concept of sociological autobiography', in M.W. Riley (ed.), *Sociological Lives*. Newbury Park, CA: Sage.

Middleton, H. (1978) 'A Marxist at Wattie Creek: fieldwork among Australian aborigines', in C. Bell and S. Encel (eds), *Inside the Whale: Ten Personal Accounts of Social Research*. Oxford: Pergamon Press.

Miller, N. and Morgan, D. (1993) 'Called to account: the CV as an autobiographical practice', *Sociology*, 27 (1): 133–43.

Mills, C.W. (1970) *The Sociological Imagination*. Harmondsworth: Penguin.

Moch, S.D. (2000a) 'The researcher experience in health care research' in S.D. Moch and M.F. Gates (eds), *The Researcher Experience in Qualitative Research*. London: Sage.

Moch, S.D. (2000b) 'The research experience as described in published reports', in S.D. Moch and M.F. Gates (eds), *The Researcher Experience in Qualitative Research*. London: Sage.

Moch, S.D. and Gates, M.F. (2000a) 'Introduction: what about the researcher experience?' in S.D. Moch and M.F. Gates (eds), *The Researcher Experience in Qualitative Research*. London: Sage.

Moch, S.D. and Gates, M.F. (eds) (2000b) *The Researcher Experience in Qualitative Research*. London: Sage.

Moore, R. (1977) 'Becoming a sociologist in Sparkbrook', in C. Bell and H. Newby (eds), *Doing Sociological Research*. London: George Allen and Unwin.

Morgan, D.H.J. (1982) 'The British Association scandal: the effect of publicity on a sociological investigation', in R.G. Burgess (ed.), *Field Research: a Sourcebook and Field Manual*. London: Unwin Hyman.

Murray, R. (2003) *How To Survive Your Viva*. Maidenhead: Open University Press.

Newby, H. (1977) 'Appendix: editorial note', in C. Bell and H. Newby (eds), *Doing Sociological Research*. London: George Allen and Unwin.

Nicolaus, M. (1972) 'The professional organization of Sociology: a view from below', in R. Blackburn (ed.), *Ideology in Social Science: Readings in Critical Social Theory*. London: Fontana.

Okely, J. (1992) 'Anthropology and autobiography: participatory experience and embodied knowledge', in J. Okely and H. Callaway (eds), *Anthropology and Autobiography*. London: Routledge.

Okely, J. (1994) 'Thinking through fieldwork', in A. Bryman and R.G. Burgess (eds), *Analyzing Qualitative Data*. London: Routledge.

Okely, J. and Callaway, H. (eds) (1992) *Anthropology and Autobiography*. London: Routledge.

O'Leary, Z. (2004) *The Essential Guide to Doing Research*. London: Sage.

Oliver, P. (2004) *Writing Your Thesis*. London: Sage.

Ormerod, P. (2004) 'Jumping off: how to leave academe', *How To Get Promoted: A Career Guide for Academics* (Booklet). *The Times Higher Education Supplement*, 19 November.

Park, R.E. (1928) 'Human migration and marginal man', *American Journal of Sociology*, 33 (6): 881–93.

Platt, J. (1976) *Realities of Social Research*. London: Sussex University Press/ Chatto and Windus.

Potter, S. (ed.) (2002a) *Doing Postgraduate Research*. London: Sage.

Potter, S. (2002b) 'Getting going', in S. Potter (ed.), *Doing Postgraduate Research*. London: Sage.

Potter, S. (2004) 'How to write up policy research', in S. Becker and A. Bryman (eds), *Understanding Research for Social Policy and Practice*. Bristol: The Policy Press.

Punch, K.F. (2000) *Developing Effective Research Proposals*. London: Sage.

Ramazanoğlu, C. with Holland, J. (2002) *Feminist Methodology: Challenges and Choices*. London: Sage.

Reed-Danahay, D. (ed.) (1997) *Auto/Ethnography: Rewriting the Self and the Social*. Oxford: Berg.

Reinharz, S. (1992) *Feminist Methods in Social Research*. Oxford: Oxford University Press.

Rex, J. and Moore, R. (1967) *Race, Community and Conflict*. Oxford: Oxford University Press.

Richardson, A., Jackson, C. and Sykes, W. (1990) *Taking Research Seriously: Means of Improving and Assessing the Use and Dissemination of Research*. London: HMSO (Department of Health).

Richardson, L. (1990) *Writing Strategies: Reaching Diverse Audiences*. London: Sage.

Riley, M.W. (ed.) (1988) *Sociological Lives*. London: Sage.

Roberts, B. (2002) *Biographical Research*. Buckingham: Open University Press.

Roberts, C.M. (2004) *The Dissertation Journey*. London: Corwin Press.

Robson, B. (2002) *Real World Research* (2nd edn). London: Blackwell.

Rose, D. (1990) *Living the Ethnographic Life*. London: Sage.

Rudestam, K.E. and Newton, R.R. (1992) *Surviving Your Dissertation*. London: Sage (2nd edn, 2000).

Rugg, G. and Petre, M. (2004) *The Unwritten Rules of PhD Research*. Maidenhead: Open University Press.

Seale, C. (ed.) (2004) *Social Research Methods: A Reader*. London: Routledge.

Seale, C., Gobo, G., Gubrium, J.F. and Silverman, D. (eds) (2004) *Qualitative Research Practice*. London: Sage.

Shaffir, W.B. and Stebbins, R.A. (eds) (1991) *Experiencing Fieldwork: An Inside View of Qualitative Research*. London: Sage.

Silverman, D. (2000) *Doing Qualitative Research: A Practical Handbook*. London: Sage.

Sociology (1993) 'Special Issue: Biography and Autobiography in Sociology', 27 (1).

Sparkes, A.C. (2000) 'Autoethnography and narratives of self: reflections on criteria in action', *Sociology of Sport Journal*, 17: 21–45.

Sparkes, A.C. (2002) *Telling Tales in Sport and Physical Activity: A Qualitative Journey*. Leeds: Human Kinetics.

Stacey, M. (1960) *Tradition and Change: A Study of Banbury*. London: Oxford University Press.

Stacey, M., Batstone, E., Bell, C. and Murcott, A. (1975) *Power, Persistence and Change: A Second Study of Banbury*. London: Routledge Kegan Paul.

Stanley, L. (1992) *The Auto/Biographical 'I': The Theory and Practice of Feminist Auto/Biography*. Manchester: Manchester University Press.

Stanley, L. (1993) 'On auto/biography in sociology', *Sociology*, 27 (1): 41–52.

Stebbins, R.A. (1991) 'Do we ever leave the field?: notes on secondary fieldwork involvements', in W.B. Shaffir and R.A. Stebbins (eds), *Experiencing Fieldwork: An Inside View of Qualitative Research*. London: Sage.

Strauss, A., Legewie, H. and Schervier-Legewie, B. (2004) 'Research is hard work, it's always a bit suffering: therefore, on the other side research should be fun', 'Anselm Strauss in conversation with H. Legewie and B. Schervier-Legewie', *Forum: Qualitative Research*, 5 (3), http://www.qualitative-research.net/fqs-texte/3-04/04-3-22–e.htm.

Taylor, S.J. (1991) 'Leaving the field: research, relationships, and responsibilities', in W.B. Shaffir and R.A. Stebbins (eds), *Experiencing Fieldwork: An Inside View of Qualitative Research*. London: Sage.

Tedlock, B. (2000) 'Ethnography and ethnographic representation', in N.K. Denzin and Y.S. Lincoln (eds), *The Handbook of Qualitative Research* (2nd edn). London: Sage.

Thody, A. (2006) *Writing and Presenting Research*. London: Sage.

Van Maanen, J. (1988) *Tales of the Field: On Writing Ethnography*. Chicago: University of Chicago Press.

Van Maanen, J., Manning, P.K. and Miller, M.L. (1990) 'Editors' introduction', in D. Rose, *Living the Ethnographic Life*. London: Sage.

Walliman, N.S.R. (2000) *Your Research Project*. London: Sage.

Ward, A. (2002) 'The writing process', in S. Potter (ed.), *Doing Postgraduate Research*. London: Sage.

Webb, E.J., Cambell, D.T., Schwartz, R.D. and Sechrest, L. (1966) *Unobtrusive Measures: Nonreactive Research in the Social Sciences*. Chicago: Rand McNally.

Whyte, W.F. (1955) *Street Corner Society* (2nd edn). Chicago: University of Chicago Press (first published in 1943).

Whyte, W.F. (1970) 'Reflections on my work', in I.L. Horowitz (ed.), *Sociological Self-Images: A Collective Portrait*. Oxford: Pergamon Press.

Whyte, W.F. (1992) 'In defence of *Street Corner Society*', *Journal of Contemporary Ethnography*, 21 (1): 52–68.

Wilkins, R. (1993) 'Taking it personally: a note on emotions and autobiography', *Sociology*, 27 (1): 93–100.

Wilkinson, D. (2005) *The Essential Guide to Postgraduate Study*. London: Sage.

Yow, V.R. (2005) *Recording Oral History: A Guide for the Humanities and Social Sciences* (2nd edn). Walnut Creek, CA: AltaMira Press.

INDEX

3